CONTENTS

Acknowledgements

I'm indebted.

I will never forget the call from Carole asking if I'd write this book. It has been an honor from start to finish. Many thanks to the wonderful crew at KMOX and to those who helped within the St. Louis Cardinal's organization. Your interest fed the fire.

I am grateful for my good friend, Doug Ferguson, who critiqued the grammar and structure. Dwight and Carol and Lynette at Hardbound completed the team it took to pull this off. They made the process exceptionally fun.

It was too amazing to actually have Mark McGwire calling for me at my office. I have erected a monument as to where I was sitting when the call came in! He was very gracious to accept our invitation to write an endorsement.

How could I ever say enough about what it was like to work beside Carole Buck? She has been delightful...every step of the way. Plus, I got to eat at J-Buck's every time I came to St. Louis....my new favorite restaurant.

Finally, I am most grateful to God and His grace that would have allowed the perfect timing for me to be a part of this work. I hope the efforts in this writing will encourage many to look His direction with sincere hearts.

Terry Rush

$\mathcal{F}$OREWORD

Voice of Silver, Heart of Gold is a labor of love to all the fans who listened and who became a part of Cardinal baseball, of KMOX radio. Your family and ours melded together.

At the end of Jack's life we read these letters to him during his courageous battle for life during his last six-months at Barnes Jewish Hospital. They carried us—they carried him. One by one, broadcast by broadcast, connection by connection, he loved you. The cards and letters came pouring in—encouraging us, praying for us, recounting your stories of how he became a part of your life. You described him as a father figure, a friend, and a part of a relationship you shared with your mother, father, or grandfather.

When you heard him you listened and learned and laughed—you wrote about your feelings. I didn't want you to think your part didn't matter. It did. It lifted him up and inspired him to the end of his life. It carried us through his death and after.

Thank you for your time and love and sharing. Thank you for the most touching trip from Twin Oaks Presbyterian Church—down Interstate 55 to Jefferson Barracks! The Interstate was closed and people were lined along the bridges and exit ramps. Our family saw you applauding, or saluting, or standing with your hands over your hearts as the hearse rolled by. Workers coming out of businesses to wave with respect to a man's tireless hours and the inability to say "No." Thank you.

By transistor radio the Voice of summer filtered its way into dark kitchens or under pillows or onto porches. Mixing were the sounds of crickets, baseball, barbeques, laughter of parents and kids—old and young, sick and well—we all had common ground: Cardinal baseball— the Cardinal Nation.

I chose Terry Rush to write this book sprinkled with your letters. I met him at a Cardinal fantasy camp where he was preaching in chapel. We became instant friends. Terry is a minister...a shepherd with an understanding of how God uses us in each other's lives if we will listen and let Him.

Sprinkled throughout this volume you may catch glimpses of some of your very own words. If they aren't your words, they surely are many of your sentiments. Don't be surprised as we pause intermittently to open an envelope containing a lovely note sent to us. It just might be yours. Not all letters received made it into this work. Please understand the family treasured every gesture of love sent our way.

All of your letters were read. I didn't want to lose track of these gifts as they are of great importance to us. You reap what you sow. God sends people into our lives right when we need them. He sent us you.

As Jack would say, thanks for your time, this time, 'til next time. So long.

Love,

Carole Buck

Carole Buck

Fans Are Applauded

Fans of St. Louis...I salute you.

Where would professional baseball be without the legacy of the St. Louis Cardinals and their outstanding fans? I knew a little about the Cardinals, but not a lot. It turned out to be one of the greatest days of my life when I found I had been traded to the St. Louis Cardinals. At first I assumed it was just a brief stop on my way to some other team at the end of the season. Not so. When I took my first step onto the field at Busch Stadium, I knew it was the best move. One factor changed my perspective, my career, and my life.....the fans of St. Louis.

The fans were the reason I stayed in St. Louis for the remainder of my career. I never in my life met fans like you. My stay in St. Louis was the first time in my career I felt appreciated for who I am. So many go through their entire life in baseball and never understand what we Cardinal players experience. The citizens didn't just love me because I was a homerun hitter or an All-Star. They genuinely cared for me as a person. It felt so good. I'll never fail to be appreciative for the love and respect given me.

And, Jack Buck? What Carole and Terry have put together is an honor the fans deserve. Everyone loved Jack. You poured out your hearts in admiration for the one who surely was the Voice of Silver with a Heart of Gold. You knew you had a champion in your midst...every season...for five decades. Jack was a man whose friendship I personally treasure.

To every baseball enthusiast who travels near St. Louis, you MUST see a Cardinal game. It is the only place in the country where you find a true baseball game and true baseball fans.

Mark McGwire

You, the fan, are hereby presented with the

FAN OF THE YEAR AWARD

"Pardon me, while I stand and applaud!" Mark McGwire just hit his 61st home run.

By the family of Jack Buck

Joe and Ann
Natalie and Trudy

Beverly and Mike
Micah and Nick

Julie and Jeff
Jack, Matt, and Ben

Christine and David
Taylor and Spencer

Dan and Carrie

Betsy and Joe
Sarah

Bonnie
Rita

Jack and Dana
Angela, Allison, Jack, Ashley, and Abby

INTRODUCTION

You, the fan, are hereby presented with the

FAN OF THE YEAR AWARD

By the family of Jack Buck

Thank you for touching so many lives with your never-ending compassion and heart of gold. You made such a difference. You're A Winner!!

Jim, Debbie, Mikayla, & Michael Kuntzman

If Charles Lindburgh is the "Spirit of St. Louis", Jack Buck is the "Inspiration of St. Louis". Voice of Silver—Heart of Gold illustrates how a slender-framed man could single-handedly arrest the hearts of St. Louisans, along with neighboring communities. He did not hunt us down. We voluntarily surrendered to his charm. He was quite effective as a one-man posse holding us captive in the Cardinal nation. We still draw to him. He remains a magnet of good.

Jack absolutely loved the fans. During an interview in the latter part of his illustrious career, Jack credited the listeners, "After all these years, I realize that my energy comes from the people at the other end."

This book is for the fans. It salutes you. It respects you. It thanks you. Voice of Silver, Heart of Gold has been written to honor you. Carole Buck has been devoted to seeing this project completed because the fans are noticeably important. There are coffee table books and library books, but she felt another book was needed....just for you. She wanted, somehow, to tell you that you make a huge difference.

Voice of Silver——Heart of Gold is intended to give you, the fans, a standing ovation for your kindness, love, and support during Jack's career, his illnesses, and his final days. Your love is noticed. The family read your notes. They heard your comments on talk shows. From Bellevue, Illinois to Ontario, Canada, to Houston, Texas, callers waited on radio talk-lines for hours to add their twist to the life of our beloved friend.

Voice of Silver—Heart of Gold is a about a tender-hearted man.....and his reciprocal-hearted fans. His was most assuredly a voice of distinction. The mid-West grew up on corn, potatoes, and the voice of Jack Buck calling the mesmerizing games of the St. Louis Cardinals.

For five decades Missouri children, and beyond, were trained in reading, 'riting, 'rithmetic and two other fundamentals. Surely our ears were trained to hear Mom's call to dinner.........and Jack Buck's crystal-clear description of the crouched stance of The Man or the intimidation of The Mad Hungarian or the nimble summersault of The Wizard.

But, Jack Buck was more than a voice. His heart had an insatiable appetite for seeing that people were treated well. Lob one small rock to the center of any farm pond, and the ripples reach in all directions. It seems God lobbed Jack Buck into the center-city of America. The ripples span the nation and beyond.....they are still reaching the shores of our hearts.

This scrapbook of love notes results. It is the family's deepest wish to form something that would honor the fans that have filled the stadium year after year—decade upon decade. What you do is important. May each of you feel as you have just been presented with the "Fan of the Year" award. You deserve it.

Terry Rush

CHAPTER ONE

A HEART
OF
FRIENDSHIP

I spent many lonely nights on farm tractors where my only contact with the world was listening to you and Mr. Shannon. Primarily, during planting season and early harvest, when we sometimes worked all night, you kept me going. I felt a part of something that was very special. I eagerly waited the time you came on the air because I knew, even though I have never met you, that you were my friend.

E. Richard Webber

What the United States District Judge wrote in the above note is typical of every Cardinal fan. We all knew Jack Buck to be our friend. We wanted him to like us. Why were we surprised when we discovered he did? He more than liked us. He lived to see that the fans were given supreme attention.

He had a welcoming spirit. Whether bumping into him at the mall or getting off an elevator at the stadium, Jack was consistent with his warm greetings and his genuine interest. He didn't just answer the phone. He cared about whoever was calling.

I once called Carole on a Saturday morning to confirm the delivery of a book I sent. When Jack answered the phone from their Spring Training condo in Jupiter, he asked who was calling. "Carole, it's for you. Terry Rush from Tulsa." And while she made her way to the phone he was inquiring, "Terry, tell me about tomorrow's sermon." In the smallest ways he perpetually let us know he was never so interrupted that he could not take the time to be courteous........and interested.

Jack Buck befriended us with relentless optimism. He was unaware of an alternative. His heart was wild to see the injured or the lonely or the struggling be benefited. In all of his seventy-seven years, his untamed heart for the benefit of the underdog was never restricted. Thank you, God!

Jack was not stumped by the puzzles life offered. Rather, he saw them as riddles of opportunities to be answered. He assumed his participation in our lives would help. And...it did.

> While some wear why-focals, Jack seemed to have an optimistic implant.

Jack Buck was one of the most unique individuals God ever created. He was handsome. He was hilarious. He was generous. He was talented. He was a good human being.

Respectful and respected were his double-edged sword. What you thought he was like....he was even more. The master of all masters of ceremonies, he excelled everywhere he turned. He possessed an instinctive slant enabling him to find the good buried beneath all the bad. While some wear why-focals, Jack seemed to have an optimistic implant.

Society can be found to be oblivious to its own needs. Passing by or scooting over, the masses make noble effort to politely stay out of each other's way. Jack risked the opposite by intentionally bumping into us. He would slip into one's unsuspecting moment only to retreat as a thief. There to rob? No, rather to bless. Jack Buck was Robin Hood with one exception. He did not rob the rich to give to the poor. He took from his own account and tossed it cheerfully to the winds of community need.

If you say Cystic Fibrosis Foundation in the St. Louis area....you might as well have said Jack Buck. He was a courageous advocate of this important team. His optimistic spirit always went bursting through their office doors to be a part of a highly dedicated group of workers devoted to putting a stop to such an invasive disease.

I want to thank you for all the efforts you have put into fundraising for the Cystic Fibrosis Foundation. Without your efforts I'm sure many of the discoveries and medicine available would not be in use right now. I appreciate the hard work.

Adam Brockmiller

> He found incredible delight in finding reason to bless instead of curse.

And then the note from another fan, Renee Havem, emphasizes the value placed upon Jack's efforts. *I got the pleasure of meeting Jack many years ago at the baseball game for the CFF. Thanks to Jack and all of his hard work with CF, I believe he has helped me live a full life.* Renee is a CF patient of more than thirty years.

Jack did not distinguish himself because he hit the ground running. No. Rather, he approached the community as a white tornado; a great and powerful whirlwind of construction, rather than destruction. It was his resolve to see that good happened to everyone within reach. He was born to fly. He found incredible delight in finding reason to bless instead of curse.

Jack Buck indeed soared.

He didn't get his wings because he necessarily excelled in academics nor because he trained with perfect discipline. Jack had wings because he thought God gave them to him. He assumed he was to use them.....and use them he did. He ascended beyond the limits of the sky as an instrument to bless as much of God's creation as he possibly could. And.....he did.

Jack was capable of causing to whomever he was speaking feel that they must be the most important person on earth. The voice of silver was an excellent listener. It was not a gimmick to draw public favor. He cared. He did not work the fans. He worked for the fans.

Optimistic? Oh, yeah. He didn't have to work at being that way. That's simply how he saw life. He *saw* life. While the multitudes may miss life when looking straight at it, Jack's eyes could see the hope of life in so many, if even discouraging, settings. He believed in people. He believed people into goodness and productivity. We are blessed with the memories.

Dear Jack,

Thank you for all the great memories since 1966, the year we moved to this area. Summer and baseball will never be quite the same without you. Even when we watched games on TV, we would listen to you on the radio.

When we would be camping in the north woods of Minnesota when our kids were young, we listened to you and Cardinal baseball, sitting around the campfire.

We felt like you and your family were part of our extended family. I think everyone felt a personal connection with you. Thank you for serving our country so valiantly in WWII. Your incredible poem written and delivered after 9-11 brought me to tears and is something I will always treasure. You were the best. All the best to your family.

I love you.....Beverly Lawrence

CHAPTER TWO

A HEART
THAT OPENED

When I think of it now, I realize that Jack also helped mold so much in me. The memories are so many——Stan the Man at old Busch Stadium; Flood, Brock, and Gibson; Ozzie; Mac! The left field bleachers are my second home. Jack was my "father" at this home away from home.

Ed Wright

One reason for such an intense relationship with Jack Buck is Cardinal fans knew he absolutely delighted in us. A-l-o-o-f does not spell Jack Buck. He mixed with us and while he was with us he handed out respect. He gave from resources we may not have possessed. Because he has given to us, we have something to pass along.

It was 1962 and Jack was doing his usual live broadcast from the famed restaurant, Stan and Biggies. Of course, the place was crowded. They came, after all, to eat at this fine dining establishment. Kathy Clase and her family were celebrating her sixteenth birthday. Jack noticed the family party and before Kathy knew it....she was being interviewed "on-the-air". Of course, she was for-the-rest-of-her-life honored. He had such a flair for connecting with the fans all about him.

> How he yet inspires us to build our communities one heart at a time.

When the interview was over, he noticed her little brother, who was also named Jack. One would think that to have offered such a surprise interview to a 16 year old would have been generosity enough. But not with Jack. He called to 8 year old Jack and inquired as to when his birthday might be. "July 22nd", beamed the youngster.

The grade-schooler was then given specific instructions to be at the park sometime near that date and Mr. Buck would take him into the dugout for his birthday. On July 21st the entire family was met by Jack. He escorted the celebrated one into the dugout and a picture was taken of Jack Clase standing beside Ken Boyer, Stan Musial, and Jack Buck.

It is little wonder Jack knew a winner when he saw one. He was one. What set Jack apart from many of us was his tenacity to act on a need. While some may tend to hear of challenging situations, Jack had a clear vision to take action. He got things done! How he yet inspires us to build our communities one heart at a time.

Was this guy Superman? He may not have been. But he was a great Clark Kent in the newsroom at least. He moved about from one important role to another. He could briskly enter a tough situation and leave having brought hope to a new level.

While at a banquet Red Schoendienst told Jack about a little 9 year old boy who had suffered burns over 98% of his body. Having fulfilled his emcee responsibilities, Jack left the hotel immediately to visit young John who was near death's door. This little one was a huge baseball fan; knew all the Cardinals' stats, and loved the players. To have Jack Buck walk into his room was a combination of surprise, shock, and impossibility.

Jack entered the room and said,

> "John, I want you to fight. I want you to fight. I want you to pull through this. And if you do, I promise you we will have a John O'Leary Day at the ballpark. You can sit in the booth with me. You hang in there and fight. "

John obeyed the command of this emcee turned motivational coach. With this charge, John began to fight his way back. His determination was focused for Jack Buck had struck....or was it Clark Kent? John hung in there and fought for many months.

About a year later John O'Leary sat in the booth with Jack Buck. Both kept their promise. In his grand style of genuine compassion, Jack stayed in touch with the burn victim. John eventually graduated from St. Louis University. Jack gave him a crystal baseball he received upon being inducted into Cooperstown.

Interaction was such a gift from Jack to his fans. He had a way of letting humility proceed. His modest nature was disarming. He defused our rattled nerves and our disjointed tongues so we could carry on some sort of decent conversation with him. But, he had to help us. Usually, we were shook. We could tell he was on our side. We always knew that. Jack Buck rooted for the fan; especially when we were in his presence.

> *I met Jack once outside the Regal Riverfront Hotel during the 1997 Winter Warm Up. I was 22 and in absolute awe. I stopped and stammered, "You're Jack Buck!" He laughed and said, "Yes, but you shouldn't look so surprised." He shook my hand, spoke to me, and thanked me for my kind words and support. That is a time I will always remember because for such an extraordinary person, he was amazingly humble and sweet.*

> *Misty Ann Donald*

He had no need to be first. Therefore, he always was. He never demanded our loyalty. Therefore, he always had it. When slugger Mark McGwire had Maris' home-run record in sight, some felt Jack should be positioned to make the history-making call each time McGwire came to the plate. It was suggested that normal patterns of the announcing rotation between Mike and Jack be altered so Jack could be the one to describe the celebrated arc over the fence.

Such suggestions fell upon the deaf, selfless ears of Jack. He would have none of that. And, as fate would have it, Mr. Shannon was the one whom the call befell. Such was the style of Jack Buck. He was not jealous, did not brag. He was not arrogant.

He and his fans had unquenchable rapport. They shared a mutual admiration society all of their own. Fred Georg pointed out that *JackBuckSt.LouisCardinals*, he believed for forty-six years, was all one word. Well, isn't it?

Although his award-winning accomplishments as a professional are worthy of superlative and lengthy description, it was his steadfast compassion for the underdog that caused this humble man to rise to achievement well beyond his ability. Whether by intention or osmosis, he inherently understood God's truth that if one will give himself away, joy inexpressible will follow.

Jack gave so much away, he hardly knew what to do with all the happiness God gave him.

Carole once asked her husband what he would say to God when he met Him. Jack quickly replied, "Why have you been so good to me?" The "why" is answered in the biblical foundation that one reaps what one sows. Jack Buck sowed graciousness, kindness, consideration, and genuine love. In a world of takers and drainers, this man was a reservoir of a giver. He lived to give.

To this day it is common to find an abundance of fans who feel very close to this celebrated icon.....truly connected. They view Mr. Buck either as a father-figure or brother or neighbor next door.

> As I grew, my desire to be near my dad was made easier if we could go to a ballgame, watch it on television or listen to the radio. Hundreds of summer nights ended with my dad slapping my knee with joy as Jack Buck shouted, "And that's a winner". I became so familiar with Mr. Buck's voice that I remember asking my father if that was grandpa telling us about the game on radio.

> *Patrick Fenton*

18

If Jack made your day, you added purpose to his life. He loved the game.
He lived for the people. His influence has no borders. He was brave. He was
witty. He was dedicated. Most of all, he was crazy about people.

He was so funny, wasn't he? "I tell people I'll probably die in the booth,"
Jack would quip, People will say, "Did you hear? Jack Buck died in the booth last
night." And they'll say, "That's too bad…who won?" Whether his hilarious one-
liners, his tearful salute to our Armed Forces, his succinct play by play of a close
call, or his recitation of a new poem just fresh off the heart, Jack Buck was a man
we wanted to love.

Spare the unnecessary coercion. We volunteered upon our own motivation.
We were crazy about this man. When the PA system at Target Greatland just off
of Highway 40 carried the announcement that Jack Buck was in the store, there
was at least one woman who went "out of her mind" with elation. Mary Kay
Severtsen could hardly believe her ears. She scrambled to gather both her 7 and 9
year olds. They dropped what they were doing and rushed to get in line for
autographs.

Mary Kay was super-enthused….no, make that hyper-enthused……so much
so that when they got through the line she got back in line……..so she could meet
him just one more time.

How true it is. Fans didn't first go crazy over the Wizard's home run, did
they? They were already crazy over their man who made the call!

Jack Buck raised
over a million dollars
for backstopper.
This award was
given to Jack by
Eric Kiell assistant chief
of Hazelwood Fire Dept
June 6, 2001

My BackYard and Jack

What a day for baseball
The sun is high
The breeze is soft
The sky, a spectacular blue

I hear a man in the background
Hawking peanuts
And another, "Cold Beer!"
The smell of fresh cut grass
And of hot dogs tantalize my nose

Out on the field, I can see my beloved Cardinals
Hernandez, Forsch, Reitz, McBride
Brock, and more
I see every pitch and every play
As if I'm there

I turn my head and look at my dad
I smile, as we sit on our back porch
Jack and KMOX took us to the game again

Carpe Diem,
Tom

"Try not, do or do not, there is no try"

CHAPTER THREE

A HEART
OF VISION

I am deeply saddened by the fact that my children will never sit on the porch on a warm summer's night and listen as the Cardinals play with nothing more than Mr. Buck's description, excitement and love of the game. It was better than being there.

Leann Wilke

How we can learn. How we do learn from this man's boundless kindness. He cared. Being considerate was neither a timely nor extra-curricular act that Jack could muster in order to impress. He was not conveniently "on" for others to make note of his charitable gestures. It was his life which flowed from his heart of gold.

A fan hung around after the game hoping to snag an autograph or two as the ballplayers left Busch. He waited. Then he waited some more. No ballplayers ever passed by. It was very late. Suddenly, Jack broke through the doors. His late night appearance seemed to confess the day had also been very long for him. Parkinson's had visibly escalated the fatigue. Yet, true to his heart of gold, Jack gladly gave his autograph... with this extraordinary inscription, *Thanks for waiting,*

> He exploited interruption by honoring the one encountered.

Jack Buck.

One surely notices how much good Jack did with such brief moments. True, the brevity of the moment may be only a wink of time, but the glorious memory lasts forever. He exploited interruption by honoring the one encountered. Fans were not a bother. We were his life.

Casey Barton of Venice, Florida tells of a most delightful account of finding himself a little short on cash. Jack came to his rescue.

The summer of 1969 I was 12 years old and me and my friend would catch the Red-Bird Express at the corner of Flora Avenue and Big Bend Blvd. in Maplewood for 50 cents to ride to the game. We would head up to Manchester and head into the city to Broadway. The bus would let us off on the south side of the Stadium and we could smell and hear the ballpark. Scorecard 25 cents, hats $4.50, peanuts 50 cents, sodas $1.00, programs $1.50, and general admissions seat $1.50. All together we could go to the ball game and come back home for $10.25 if we got everything. We were kids and we got it all (that money was burning a hole in our pocket from cutting grass, I had $10.00).

It was going to be a great day, Gibby was pitching against Marichal. It was a great game just being able to see Gibby pitch (the year before I was in the left field bleachers when the finest pitching performance was ever pitched in the World Series. Game 1, 1968 Gibby strikes out 17 and beats McLain 4-0). When the game was over I was in trouble. I came to the park with $10.00 and I got everything and I only had 25 cents left over. I needed 50 cents for the bus ride back home. My friends had a field day with me. "You're gonna walk." "Your Dad is going to tan your hide." "See you later." And on and on.

I remember watching Mr. Buck with his family at Tropicana Bowling Lanes. He was always so nice to everyone and you could see how much he loved his family. My Mom worked at People's State Bank right next to the lanes and she would always wait on Mr. Buck when he came in. She always said he was a gentleman's gentleman.

I saw Mr. Buck coming down the street with Mr. Randolph (another wonderful St. Louisan). I went up to Mr. Buck, this was on Broadway in front of the old courthouse, and said, "Excuse me Sir, I spent all my money at the game except for 25 cents and I would like to know if I could borrow 25 cents so I could get on the bus to go home?"

He looked at me with that wonderful smile and said, "Son, did you have fun at the ball park?" I said, "Yes Sir." He said, "I am going to give you 50 cents so you have an extra quarter in case this happens again." I said, "Thank you Mr. Buck and I will pay you back." He said, "Don't worry about it." I told him, "I have to or my Mom and Dad will put me over the coals." He shook my hand and said, "Be careful getting home." I just stood there staring at my hand. I did not wash if for two days. My friends could not say a word and I had the upper hand on the ride home on that bus.

About a month later I was at the game again and we were down by where the players came out trying to get them to sign our gloves. I saw Mr. Buck and went up to him and said, "Mr. Buck, I don't know if you remember me but about a month ago you loaned me 50 cents so I could get back home on the bus." He said, "You don't need more money, do you?", and looked at me like my Dad would when I was in trouble.

There was no smile now. I said, "No Sir, I have the fifty cents I owe you." and handed it to him. He said, "You keep it in case you need it again." I said, "Mr. Buck, my Mom and Dad said no matter what, I was supposed to make you take this back." He laughed and said, "O.K."

I still have that quarter with my baseball that all the Cardinals signed for the 1968 World Series.

One can't have too many raises nor receive too many birthday wishes. Jack never had too many fans who loved him. He was connected to thousands of us—decades of us—generations of us—at the heart.

I've always associated Jack Buck with my memories of my own grandfather, who, like Jack, was a dedicated family man. At my grandfather's funeral, I gave a eulogy that ended with some sentiments about what I felt I had inherited from him: a sense of decency, a love for God & family, and a strong value system. I'm feeling the same way today about Jack Buck—like I've just inherited a fortune…like I'm an heir to something so much more precious and dear than money or possessions. Jack Buck left behind a great legacy….and we are ALL his heirs.

Brenda Ruzicka

While being honored at an awards banquet, Jack remarked,

"I'm grateful for the bat of Stan Musial, the arm of Bob Gibson, the legs of Lou Brock and the glove of Ozzie Smith. Turn the radio on. You'll hear a friend. You will enjoy. You will learn. You will imagine. You will improve. Turn the radio on at home, in your car, in prison, on the beach, in a nursing home. You will not be alone. You will not be lonely. Newspapers fold. Magazines come and go. Television self-destructs. Radio remains the trusted common-denominator in this nation."

While Jack Buck most certainly attracted the masses with his voice of silver, there was something about his gigantic heart of gold which surpassed all charted success. Jack could see hope. While some would intentionally avoid any who might have been regarded as a nuisance, Jack was different. He saw our potential. He convinced us we were good. He believed in us.

Jack didn't miss the opportunity to lift the spirits of a dejected fan. He wouldn't let one of need be lost in a crowd of plenty. His eyes hawked the corridors and searched the cafes. He saw people. While their voices might convince most people they were doing fine, Jack possessed a special sense to detect if the story might be otherwise.

Jack Buck was born to fly. He was a consummate pilot of life. He was a hard worker. He was too humble to be greedy. The man was high on seeing that everyone around him was benefited with hope and happiness. If there was any way he could contribute to another's good day, he got it done. He went out of his way to see us finish our day stronger than when we started.

> *While visiting with the patients at the VAMC spinal cord injury unit, Jack asked one of the guys who was about to go to the "Wheel Chair Olympics" (in Baltimore, I think) if they were going to bring back a trophy. The vet replied that they didn't have enough dollars to take all the guys who could compete.*
>
> *Jack turned to his wife and said, "Let me have the checkbook, Carole." He wrote a personal check to the Paralyzed Veterans of America for $5000 and said go rent a bus. He visited the SCI unit often and always thanked the vets for what they had done!*
>
> *Ray Timm*

Jack was charismagnetic. Neither his position nor his skill brought him his entire fame. The aroma of his brilliance truly arises from repetitive deeds of goodness toward those who needed a special pat on the back or a little burst of hope. The man couldn't (wouldn't) stop being generous.

Kevin McDaniel passed along a story of Jack and friends when in Las Vegas. Jack gave the waitress $100 tip before the meal. He asked her if it would be all right to tip in advance. The service was great. Wherever he went, he was sure to be a generous servant to those who worked hard for their living.

To be perfectly honest, I felt like a good friend as so many others must have experienced. His professionalism, work ethic, charity, and just genuine "all man" demeanor were true treasures for all St. Louis and many others throughout the country.

Warren Morgens

"Carole Buck.... I am enclosing two photos of Jack Buck and our granddaughter taken on Grandparents Day at the ballpark Sep.9, 2001. Jack was telling our granddaughter, Alex Capestany, what a pretty smile she had. The other picture is of Jack, Alex, and myself....."

CHAPTER FOUR

A HEART
FOR
INSPIRATION

We senior citizens can't get around too well, so we would listen to Jack broadcast the games in our homes. We'd make popcorn and pretend we were at the stadium.

Carol and Jerry Merz

Jack Buck didn't just take up God's created space. He lived from it to the max! One will never hear it said, *I was with Jack Buck one time and it was just awful. He was really in the pits. I didn't want to be around him.* Jack did for the world what made him come alive. He hungered to see that others benefited.

Jack Buck was an inspiring wordsmith. How he could hammer out the contours of a game upon the anvil of a microphone. His voice of silver let us into the game through our own personal gate. With succinct cadence his raspy expressions gave each of us a front row seat to every embroiled Cardinal battle. Because of his adlib-ability, truly wherever Jack sat, we sat.

I grew up listening to what was an artist's canvas. Jack would paint pictures of baseball that would rival Michelangelo. Lying in bed listening and picturing in my mind what a thrill it must have been to be in the booth looking down on home plate at Busch Stadium, it convinced me I had to someday try to paint my own picture for someone to envision.

Mark Champion

Sometimes we sat behind home plate.......through Jack, that is. At other times we stood behind second base. With the umpire we gave judgment as to whether the fan interfered with the centerfielder. Sometimes it was hard for us to tell for sure.....but we were pretty certain the fan reached into Van Slyke's glove. How really exciting it got when we would march right down there where Whitey Herzog was fussing with umpire Joe West. Ooooh. We walked right up to them both and gave our two cents worth........through Jack, that is.

Jack Buck has, for me, always been synonymous with the Cardinals. Born in 1949 and having grown up on a farm in the metro-east, it is impossible for me to think of the Cardinals without thinking of Mr. Buck. Like so many others who grew up "before TV", the Cardinals were Jack Buck on the radio on the front porch on a warm summer night.

Connie Jefferies

His skillful articulation sketched acrobatic events and painted breath-taking, close-call pictures. He was television on radio. His voice became a lens for each listener to view every inside pitch of Bob Gibson or the swift move of Willie McGee breaking from first. Because of Jack we could see the game on radio.

Jack always "took us out to the ballgame" no matter where we were.

Rosemary Jean Schaffer
Terry Sedberry

You gave to me an interest in baseball that I have kept for sixty years. Living in Southern Illinois, every summer night you made us seem as if we were at the game.
Sue Jeffords

For him there could have been crafted the words radiovision or imagi-vision. In fact, he possessed such excellent command of the grammatical palette it was not unusual for the fans to turn the volume on the TV down and tune into Jack on the radio during Cardinal games. His gravelly voice was most distinct. His was a *Voice of Silver.*

Jack's voice was unique. There was a secret to why this beloved man was the distinguished pied-piper to all St. Louis fandom. They would high-five grandmother if he declared Joe Cunningham safe at home.   With equal delight they would elbow a friend's ribcage at first glimpse of an approaching punch-line during a banquet speech. The word-weaver was adored. Some in life are famous. But few are famous and so lovingly cherished. Jack was both.

Jack Buck had a *Voice of Silver* because his speech was endowed by a *Heart of Gold.* He found no satisfaction in saying "things". He was called to express "life". He could create something out of nothing. We soaked it up. Jack was on a mission of whom he never tired….delight the fan. Jack was alive. Therefore, each descriptive play was a simple brushstroke upon the canvas of our minds. We got the picture.

The New Testament reveals that from the abundance of a man's heart his mouth speaks. There was the Voice of Silver only because its backing was Jack's Heart of Gold. Indeed he had a job. His interest, though, was people. His words could captivate a crowd or charm an individual. He was equally interested in both.

And so it is. Fans. Fans who have been influenced by this unusual man. He calls out the good in others. He causes us to want to try harder. He edges us closer to believing the good within ourselves. He inspires some to serve God by being responsive to others.

For all u do Jack, we will miss u.   Of all the great calls, your getting me involved in the Backstoppers and your Christmas party at home was tops. This is now a part of our family tradition.

Jeff and Marsha Hader

One part of Jack's expertise tips us off as to this sensitive heart; his poetry. In order to be an effective poet, one needs a combined creativity with words and sensitivity of people. Again, this man had it in abundance. His timing was good. His tempo was crisp. His focus was accurate. While some have neither rhyme nor reason to life......
...Jack had both. He formed words to fortify people.

> He edges us closer to believing the good within ourselves.

Note his combination of brilliance and simplicity as he finds a way to put mankind in order through A Perfect World.

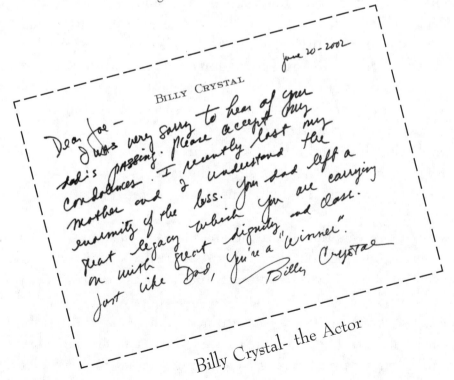

Billy Crystal- the Actor

A Perfect World

A gentleman came home from work one evening,
sat down to read the paper and relax.
But his six year old had other ideas
and one hundred questions to ask.

The father put up with the boy for awhile,
then called for some help from his wife.
He was told he was on his own till they dined
and he should share in the family life.

A thought unfurled—
He knew what to do to keep the youngster quiet.
On page ten he saw a map of the world.
It was a crazy idea…but he'd try it.

He tore page ten into many pieces,
told his son to put the map back together.
He started to read the paper again,
first the sports then the weather.

A few minutes later the father received
one of the greatest shocks of his life.
The youngster stood there—
and the map was perfect.
He let out a yell for his wife.

They both were informed
there was a picture of a boy
in the paper—on page nine,
and the little guy knew if he put the boy together right,
the world would turn out fine.

Jack's Heart of Gold overflowed from America's center-city into neighboring states, nations, and yes, even continents. If his powerful influence could not be restricted by geography, neither could it be contained by any one generation. He was adored by the young and old. How many accounts are given of those who were thankful to grandparents, parents, or aunts or uncles who groomed their young to keep their ears tuned to the silver voice of summer.

When Jack was restrained to his hospital bed, words of encouragement poured in.

Dear Jack,

Hopefully this note gets to you in good spirits and gaining strength everyday. I must tell you I owe you a word of thanks for a nice gesture you made to a group of McDonnell Douglas people who were down in Florida during spring training. You went out of your way to take these guys out to dinner which was truly a thrill for them.

Sincerely,
Jack Sheehan
McDonnell Douglas Retired

Dear Carole,

This picture was taken of Jack with four of our six children at the Cardinals spring training camp in St. Pete in 1984. I asked Jack if I could take his picture with our children but I couldn't gather them all quickly, so only four children made the picture.

Jack said he could not imagine staying in a condo with six kids and I laughed and said " that would be great since we are staying in a tent." My remark about put Jack away.

Judy Hamilton

Dear Family,

My age is 62, so that means I've been listening to Jack since about age 14. What a great 48 years these have been!

Although I didn't know it at the time, I think I must have heard Jack's last (or near last Cardinals game) in early October, last Fall. I believe the Cardinals were playing a night game, at Arizona. And I still marvel at how Jack ended. It was late, Iowa time, I suppose at or near midnight, and I was in bed listening to KMOX. I can still almost hear these words of Jack's:

AND SO I BID YOU FAREWELL FROM THE GREAT SOUTHWEST. FINAL SCORE: ___ ___ SO LONG EVERYBODY!

I remember thinking – what class! Those words –"the great south west." This was no ordinary sports broadcaster. 9-11 had just happened three weeks or so earlier, in New York City, Washington, DC, and in Pennsylvania. Just about all of us were still numb over the terrible 9-11 tragedy – our nation had been rocked and was still hurting.

And here's Jack, trying to lift our spirits, and telling everyone listening on the airwaves that our nation is big and it is great. Those words, "the great south west" were so timely, given in the darkness of night, and will linger in people's hearts perhaps forever.

John Francis Buck, you were more than a sports announcer – you ARE an American icon! God bless you in your new eternal home!

Respectfully,
Francis R. Lalor
Iowa City, Iowa

Dear Mr. Buck:

Throughout the years, I have listened to you describe the action of Cardinal baseball. During my high school years, it was my dream to go into the radio business and become a sports broadcaster due in large part to listening to your Cardinal broadcasts. Finances and other things known as life got in the way of the dream, but in 1989, you provided a cherished memory for me before a Sunday afternoon game, one I'll never forget.

> I collect sports memorabilia, and like a lot of kids, and adults, I was standing outside the Cardinal clubhouse waiting for players to come along so I could seek their autograph. You happened to be walking along, and a swarm of people crowded around you. I have an appreciation for the history of the game, and understand the importance of passing it along to young people. So I waited patiently as you graciously penned your name for everyone in attendance. It just so happened that I was the last person there. I recall that you said, "Thank you so for waiting." I didn't mind at all, as I had the opportunity to meet someone I'd idolized, and grown up listening to. Not only did you sign my baseball, but you spent about five minutes of your valuable time with me.

I just wanted to thank you for taking the time to listen to a young man's dream, and for signing that ball. It is a prized part of my collection, along with the memory of meeting the gracious man who brings honor upon his craft every time he steps behind the mike.

Thank you Mr. Buck.
Sincerely,
Richard Allensworth, Jr.

CHAPTER FIVE

A HEART
OF IMPACT

So, excuse me Jack, and all other Cardinal fans, while we stand up and applaud, on a great life that has passed and a legacy that will never die.

Mike Richter

If Mark McGwire was an impact player, Jack Buck was an impact citizen. Even at his own memorial service Jack was giving direction…through his influence, that is. Overflow crowds were guided to side rooms equipped with large television monitors. An usher invited the crowd suggesting there was a section in the balcony available for seating. A young woman wearing shorts and shirt expressed reluctance as she was not appropriately dressed to sit in the balcony. The usher had obviously been groomed by the Buck-style of inclusiveness. *Mr. Buck would think you are dressed just fine.* Because of his pure lack of bias and prejudice, we could have all gotten to sit in the balcony.

Rob Young, Rob Shannan

Only days following Jack's death, one of his loyal fans was killed in an auto accident. Rob Young was 35. Inside the golden parchment brochure given those who attended his funeral is a picture of Rob and good friend Rob Shannan……along with Jack Buck in front of Busch stadium. His parents, Ronnie and Bonnie Young, wrote,

> *Rob was killed in July, 2002 in a trucking accident and the moment that Mr. Buck shared with Rob and Rob Shannan continues to be important to our family. It represents an exceptional moment in his life and the picture is now a treasure for all of us to share.*

AfterGlow

I'd like the memory of me
to be a happy one.
I'd like to leave an after glow
of smiles when life is done.
I'd like to leave an echo
whispering softly down the ways,
Of happy times and laughing
times and bright and
sunny days.
I'd like the tears of those who
grieve, to dry before the sun
Of happy moments that I leave
When life is done.

In Memory of Rob Shannan

An "exceptional moment" can be claimed by a half-century full of countless fans who loved this inspiring personality. He was too minute to have ever guessed how he touched the lives of multi-generations with such love and kindness.

Who was not moved deeply by his poem following 9/11? It was more than his poetic words that pierced our hearts. We saw the poet on national television. His drawn face cheered us on to never give up. His slender frame of a body assured us all of how frail and vulnerable to attack we are. And then he delivered poetic justice.

> Dear Jack,
> Last year, Jackie and I attended several Cardinal baseball games at Busch Stadium. However, our favorite moment from last year occurred when you read the poem about America staying united following the events of September 11. That moment was very humbling for us.
>
> Larry Waugh

The poem was penned by a poet-warrior. In them one can feel both the emotion of a veteran and kindness of a grandpa. His dual nature of desiring peace while looking the enemy in the eye is, in itself, revealing of the heart of an ambassador who lived daringly compassionate.

His capacity as broadcaster or patriot or poet....it matters not which area. We loved this man whose heart of gold had enormous range, and touched us similarly to that of a fan who wrote:

> I spent three years away in the service from 1966 thru 1969 and while I could listen to Armed Forces Radio with a small transistor banded to my helmet, the World Series in 67 and 68 wasn't the same when you couldn't recognize the voices. I became a baseball fan because of Jack and Harry and the best tribute I can make to Jack is that when I returned from overseas and as Veteran unwelcome in the country embroiled in turmoil, it was that first Cardinal game I listened to that brought me home. I remember hearing Jack and Harry's voices announcing the game and I found myself collapsing on a city curb, tears in my eyes realizing I was finally home. I am really home. I met Jack many times through the years from the days when I sold newspapers next to the KMOX studios on Hampton to events both charitable and trade, but I never got to tell him how much he meant.
>
> Tony Shaw

Jack was an advocate for all the men and women of this country who serve it well and risk their lives daily to keep our country safe.

Carole Buck,

I'm enclosing pictures of James Bauer a friend and great admirer of Jacks. He is blind and goes to the Missouri School for the Blind. This friendship for James started in 1996 when he phoned KMOX to ask questions of Jack about the Cardinals. Jack invited him to come to the ballgame and be his guest in the booth; which got him known in Jack's book, as " The Take

over the Booth Man." He then was on TV with Jack and Christine.

James wants to be on the radio talking sports; which he really knows about. He misses his voice on the radio, as he explained all the plays; that made the game real for him. He continued to stay in touch with Jack till his death.... Thank you, Dorothy Trefey (grandmother for James Bauer)

CHAPTER SIX

A HEART
FOR
PURPOSE

Jack, thank you for so many good memories—for bringing Dad and I so close. The last time Dad and I were together was in 1984—in the bleachers at Busch Stadium—listening to you on our transistor radios.

Rene'

Jack Buck lived a life of which others dream. His life had meaning. While frustration plagues the multitude because they can't find their niche, Jack knew exactly what he was about. He knew where he was going. His pursuit was fearless. Therefore, he experienced a life that comes from the deep regions of God's creation.

> While countless ones are paralyzed upon the shores of opportunity, Jack would set sail.

While countless ones are paralyzed upon the shores of opportunity, Jack Buck would set sail. Crowds didn't intimidate. Strangers caused him no hesitation. Failure was no threat. It only moved him closer to the next success. If a job was lost he was only closer to finding the next great horizon. The more his health deteriorated the greater his chances of meeting a new set of doctors and nurses that needed to hear his jokes.

It is no exaggeration. The number who care deeply about Jack Buck can only be estimated in terms of a half-century. He was an ordinary man with extraordinary senses. He seemed to always make a connection. He was good to everyone he met.

If Will Rogers never met a man he didn't like, Jack never met a person he didn't esteem higher than himself. He revered us. For those who may have had reason to have felt low on the totem pole of worth, his attention became even more riveting; more necessary. Everybody was somebody important to Jack Buck. His life shows it.

Paulette McFarland tells of her first parent/teacher night at her son's new school. Since she knew no one, she was terribly uneasy. Paulette stood in a lengthy line of parents. Increasingly she felt more alone in the crowd; more uncomfortable. Quietly, she asked God if he would help her rid the feelings of inferiority that flooded her heart.

And just that quick I heard a voice. A voice I'd heard more than even my own father's voice. A voice that calmed me, that made me smile, that reminded me of the big picture...... was coming from behind me. I remember turning around with relief and thanking God as I knew someone after all.

It was Jack.

One man contacted KMOX to share his story of how Jack touched his life. One Christmas he was down on his luck and staying in a public shelter. Unannounced, Jack showed up giving out clothes and money. "I was lucky enough to be one to help bring in the clothes from his car." Jack gave him a twenty dollar bill and the man used that money to buy his daughter a Christmas present. The man got out of the shelter one week later. Referring to Jack, and those like him, he wrote, "He who serves others is truly a great man." Jack was a giant of a leader because he served others.

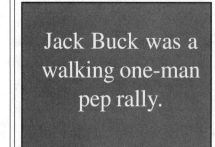

Jack Buck was a walking one-man pep rally.

Jack had a purpose in life while many wish for one……. but remain clueless as to what it may be. Jack had more than a job. He had a ministry. And, he knew it. He was about people. The occupation of being a world-famous broadcaster merely served as a tool for him to get to do what he really loved…..encouraging people to move forward and to move up. He wasn't mistaken about the greatness he sensed in others. Jack Buck was a walking one-man pep rally.

Jack Buck passed by the same people whom others passed. What begs for note of difference was his genuine interest that caused him to take positive action. He made a difference. He mingled with the crowds and could still see the individual.

Esther Nichols was a recipient of his kindness. She worked at the stadium twenty years plus with SportService Department. Following a game one Easter Sunday she was walking from the stadium to the bus-stop. Her arthritis had kicked in full blast after standing long hours on concrete serving the fans. She and Jack crossed paths. "Hello. And, have a nice day. You deserve it." Esther thanked Mr. Buck as they exchanged brief well-wishes.

Once passed, Jack called back, "Young Lady." He was walking toward her with instructions to hold out her hand. She wondered if it might be tickets to a game. Maybe a souvenir? Whatever it was, he placed it in her hand and closed her hand. He said, "Buy yourself something nice. You deserve it." and walked away. Upon opening her hand she found a one hundred dollar bill. She called out, "Sir, sir, I think you have made a mistake". He just faded into the crowd.

What made this man tick? He never assumed he was better. He did assume he had been given too much by God. He assumed whoever was near him held top honors. A four year old, introduced by his father to Jack, asked, "Are you famous?" "No, I'm not famous," Jack insisted. "Just lucky." How lucky are his fans that Jack thought it was his good fortune to be lucky.

Whether 4 years old or 84 years old, Jack was famous to a bunch of us. I don't think, though, he knew how many of us he got into trouble because when we were supposed to be sleeping, as youngsters, we'd sneak to hear the rest of the game.

As a life long Cardinal fan, I can say without a doubt that you, Mr. Buck, made me a fan. I can remember listening to you as a child when the Birds were on a West Coast swing and my dad catching me with that radio in bed.

Greg Bacon

I used to hide my AM transistor radio under my pillow after bedtime the finish hearing the game.

Kevin Grace

It was so hard to stay awake during those West Coast trips. For those who lived in the country, the signal was often impossibly weak. Jack and Harry would fade in....then they'd fade out...then we'd drift off to sleep....then we'd wake up and the signal would be strong....we'd listen awhile longer. We would repeat the cycle about six times. Often we would awaken only to find music playing and we wouldn't know what happened...who won?

Therefore one wonders if Jack knew how hard we worked as kids to be dedicated to such Cardinal fannery? We took risks. *As a young fan in the early sixties, to whom game tickets were rare and precious and the Cardinal players were only one step removed from Homeric, you were my connection. The broadcasts from sunny Al Lang Field, in St. Pete, Florida were magical—at last we had hope that warmer days were on the way. My brother and I would break out our mitts in anticipation, even though the first game of catch was still weeks away for us.*

Throughout every summer, the radio was always tuned to the Cardinal games as we followed every win and loss. And I cannot tell you how much fun it was to follow a night game from Dodger Stadium or Candlestick Park, long past our bedtimes, listening to you on all nine of our mighty transistors until we fell asleep with the radio next to the pillow (or until Dad caught us sneaking the game....).

Ward Silver

Like many other baseball fans, I remember falling asleep with the transistor radio by my pillow listening to you and Harry Caray broadcast West Coast games.

Carolyn Allen

He thought of himself as the luckiest man he ever met. I once stood in the booth during his final year of calling the Cardinal games. His body jerked and twitched. He was hurting. Yet, he ran full-steam ahead. His Parkinson's surely left him exhausted. The gravelly voice kept pumping out the charm. Although his body was breaking down, his spirit provided opportunity to bring us a smile. "I've given the Cardinals the best years of my life," Jack quipped. "Now, I'm giving them my worst."

CHAPTER SEVEN

A HEART
FOR ACTION

Going to see a Cardinal game————expensive
Listening to a game called by Jack Buck————PRICELESS!
Christine S.

Jack was so relaxed. No show. Nothing smug. He was a wonderful human being whose heart was bigger than his body. He wore the community of St. Louis like a pair of decade-old slippers....quite at home and marvelously comfortable. It was nothing for him to show up at a golf course, pick out three total strangers, form a foursome.......and have a great time.

He exuded ease. When touring Menard State Penitentiary, he delighted the inmates with his lovable and sheer presence. "Hey, Jack, can you get me a room with a view?!" called one of the inmates. "I'll do better than that, Jack volleyed, How about a skeleton key and an egg salad?"

Jack lived on the edge. Everyone was welcomed into his path. He could glide through interruption with complete poise. Bob Hope or Tony Bennett....matters not who ..Jack worked from the geography of the heart. If you weren't a celebrity to begin with, one always felt like one when Jack got done attending to your day.

Weakened by Arthrogryposis (lack of muscle in body limbs), two year old Robby Cerrioti was guided along by holding the hands of his Dad and grandmother, Aggie. Entering this scene at Lobby 300 of Busch Stadium was Jack Buck. He knelt down, hugged Robby......and cried. From that day on every opening day of the season, Jack would burst through the doors of Lobby 300 and say to grandmother Agnes (the receptionist), "Hi Aggie. How is Robby?"

Jack would always wish Robby "Happy Birthday" on April 13th. He never forgot. When he turned 13...on the 13th...Jack said hello to Robby on the radio and wished him well. After the game, Jack came through the office and Robby stood up and said, "Thank you Mr. Buck for wishing me happy birthday!" Out of earshot of grandmother and other relatives, Jack took young Robby over to a corner of the room where they could talk in private. The two whispered briefly. Afterward, Jack wished everyone a good night and left for his car.

Bobby ask his son what the two of them were talking about all by themselves. Robby said Mr. Buck gave him one hundred dollars for his birthday. "He told me not to put it in the bank, but to spend it on anything I want." The money was folded into a small square. Bobby's response was, "Son, I'm sure it's a ten; not a hundred." But Robby was right. Jack's love of this child

> He wore the community of St. Louis like a pair of decade-old slippers... quite at home and marvelously comfortable.

brought tears to the entire family.

In 2002, while Jack was hospitalized and failing, Joe Buck said during the game, "I want to wish Robby Ceriotti a happy birthday because if I don't my dad will get after me when I go to the hospital tonight."

**Jack with Robby
Ceriotti**

Recall McGwire chasing Maris' homerun record? Mark McGwire was rightly upset over an umps call in his first at bat of an important game. We all were outraged. The home plate ump ejected Mark in the first inning. The fans' loyalty went, of course, immediately to Mark. It was a rare Cardinal moment for all as great disdain was expressed over this umpiring blunder. The fans howled in disgust over the ump's blind call. And Jack was right in there with them.

Jack tossed and turned all night. How he grieved. He felt he and the crowd had behaved quite poorly. Coincidentally, the next day was "Jack Buck Day" when his Hall of Fame statue was to be unveiled at an entrance to Busch Stadium. Oh, how he regretted the attack all had made on the men in blue.

The next day he pleaded with the crowd to withdraw all animosity; to put away their swords. He expressed how inappropriate such behavior was. He called for the fans of St. Louis to show the men in blue what St. Louis fans were really like. Otherwise, it would ruin his day.

As game time drew near, the umpires approached the field. The crowd went silent........and then broke out into soft applause and then louder applause erupting into a standing ovation. Jack Buck trained Cardinal fans to think of others first.

No event better captures the pure decency of Jack Buck than his plea a couple of years ago for the fans of St. louis to welcome and cheer the umpires the day after they had ejected Mark McGwire in the first inning of a game during his home run chase. Most likely, Mr. Buck helped prevent an ugly scene that Sunday—as if a parent had schooled his 50,000 children on how to behave in class.

Steve Coleman

We feel certain that a major reason Cardinal fans are as electric, as celebrative, as we are is due to the training and leadership of Jack. His wasn't a job to describe a ball game. His was the work of molding pliable fans to the orderliness of robust and partnered cheerleaders...everyone of us.

New players starting with the Cards always talk about how great the baseball fans are in St. Louis. I believe that Jack helped to create the Cardinal fans the way they are.

Rob Roseman

By the way, Jack's special day was incredible. The fans turned out in droves to honor their favorite sportscaster of all time. He is a hero. Jack had special friend and minister, George Robertson on hand to offer a prayer. All of this is a part of who Jack Buck is. Note how beautiful and meaningful are the words offered for this public figure.

Lord Jesus,

Your presence brings joy to every occasion. Come now and be in our midst. Help us to honor a man you made in your image, a man that we love.

On this day our chief celebration is your resurrection from the dead winning victory over sin and death for anyone who would receive you as Lord and Savior. At that resurrection you gave gifts to men.

And you have given many gifts to our friend, Jack Buck. The gift of mental alacrity, verbal articulation, the ability to work hard, and a devoted family, and a generous spirit. The gifts reflect a generous God and so this day we praise you for your work to and through Jack Buck and pray for it to continue.

Each of us gathered here who is a child of yours will surely ask as Mr. Buck asks at the end of his book, "Why are you so good to us?"

May this celebration today only serve to draw us and our friend ever closer to you and for your blessing.

In Jesus name.....Amen

His action included more than being attentive to an individual in need of the moment. It took him to the front lines of leadership. He was willing to encounter ill will with transforming effectiveness. When it came to getting involved, Jack was in the lead. This merely reinforces the idea Cardinal fans are as supportive and positively demonstrative because all cheers can be traced to Jack.

Fans Start Early

CHAPTER EIGHT

A HEART
FOR GREATNESS

I worked for the St. Louis Water Company during a summer 10 years ago. A crew foreman told me that a few years prior they were repairing a water main break near the Buck's home. They saw Jack drive by and then later returned with pizza for the whole crew.

Rob Roseman

Headlines of the St. Louis Post-Dispatch, June 19, 2002:
Voice of the Cards Dies. He was the Soul of the City.

The soul of the city? How about the Soul of the entire Cardinal kingdom! Long-range influence is felt by recipients from townships, states and nations away, while the person himself merely assumed he was giving an after-dinner speech in Peoria, Illinois at the moment. Jack's seed of generosity and graciousness has sprouted and little communities of benefactors crop up; first here and then there......and then everywhere.

Jack Buck is bigger than life! How do you describe a man whose inner spirit was larger than the fame he carried about town? He was not a typical celebrity; not by a long shot. His heart never left the perch of humble beginnings. Sacred scriptures speak of the things we see as being temporary and the things not seen as eternal. While Mr. Buck did much for the community that was known, it seems his unseen spirit of benevolence wins.

The last award Jack received was St. Louis' prestigious "Citizen of the Year". Where would you guess this man would focus his remarks? Where he always walked his life. Look over a segment of his acceptance speech. After introducing his special guests and making typical Buck-style remarks he shifted with these words:

It may surprise you to hear me say that I belong up here today. But I do. Because, I am a pinch hitter for the real Citizen of the Year. Who is it? I don't know. They don't know. We don't know. But I'll tell you who it could be. It could be a teacher who today took a little extra time to help a student. It could be a fireman who tonight will carry a child to safety. It could be a parent taking care of a child with MS, with dystrophy, or cystic fibrosis. It could be a son or a daughter caring for an aging, ailing parent. It could be a person donating a kidney to a sibling, donating money to the Backstoppers, or 40 million to the symphony.

It could be a widow sending some of her social security money to the Salvation Army, or someone playing in the Salvation Army Band. It could be a person still unable to move after being shot in the neck in Vietnam thirty-two years ago. It could be somebody today that's packing sandbags to protect a river levee. Somebody doing research at St. Louis U or Washington U. A nurse staying overtime to administer a little extra tender loving care. A patient, smiling nursing home worker. A police officer responding to anybody's call for help. Someone who visits a prison and teaches the inmates how to read. Each of us in this room, and we have the world to thank, have done some of these things.

People for whom I've appreciated seeing do those wonderful things everyday, and receive a few thanks and no recognition and they keep on doing it. We thank them today. We recognize them today. It's written in the program here that I am a kind person. I hope I am. I try to be. I know what I have done. I know what I haven't done. But being a pinch-hitter today makes me very happy—despite the tears.

He never forgot he began with nothing. Neither wealth nor fame could erode his recollection of living quite meagerly as a child. Because of that, Jack almost made generosity his occupation. Late at night at the KMOX headquarters several college kids...or recent grads....would be scurrying to do their work as interns. Jack would always be shaking their hands. It was not unusual that they find he had deposited a fifty or a hundred in their palm.

When Jennifer Siess interned in '94, Jack would toss her quarters to get a soda....one for Jack and one for her. Such a trek became routine. Once he threw a bill at her and told her to get a drink for herself...he was "out o' here". She put the bill in her pocket for a later purchase. When she later dug out the paper wad, it was a hundred dollar bill.

He wanted people to know that he knew they existed. It was important to him to let others know of their importance. He never met a person who was not truly and wonderfully unique in their own special way. He worked at learning the names of everyone he worked with...including those who took out the trash.

Who cannot be awed by Jack's insistent moves of courtesy that built hearts of confidence? He was so consistent with his efforts to bless others. It was not unusual for some in the St. Louis workforce to go home and hear a message on their machine, "Hi, this is Jack Buck. I just wanted to wish you a Merry Christmas." The man was magnificently thoughtful.

One named Paul called in with this report. He took his son Trick or Treating. When they knocked on Jack's door, the duo were invited in. Jack visited with them, gave the young boy a treat...........and *thanked them* for stopping by.

Joe tells of sitting in first class on the plane as he returned to St. Louis. During the flight, a stewardess approached him asking if Jack Buck was his father. She shared with Joe how just about a year earlier Jack and Carole were on her flight out West when they suffered a delay. To help pass the time the stewardesses passed a bag collecting seating stubs along with a dollar.

One stewardess didn't want to play the game again because it was always someone in first class to win and the coach passengers always complained. Nevertheless, they conducted the drawing which could reach approximately $250. Jack's seat number was drawn. A little girl from the back of the plane presented Jack the bag of money while the coach passengers groaned at the thought of some first-classer winning again.

Jack had the little girl explain about the sack of money. He then said, "How about if I take the dollar and you take the bag of money?" The flight attendant said that was the first time that ever happened. She went on to explain that she would never forget the look on the little girl's face as one could tell her family could surely use the money. She received a letter from the family expressing how much this meant to them as the dad had lost his job and they were so encouraged by Jack's generosity.

He was so good to fans, especially kids. On one occasion he was in the Sports office at KMOX when about a dozen 8 year-olds came through on tour with their school. The tour director pointed out to the kids that in that room was the famous Jack Buck. He dropped what he was doing and came out, shook the hands of each child and fascinated them with stories for another 30 minutes.

And it wasn't that he did this to reflect upon his greatness. He was simply so interested in each one. He would tell about his work and, in turn, ask what they were doing in school and other questions to draw them in. Their eyes were as big as saucers.

Although Jack would not be physically classed as a heavy-weight, he surely packed the clout. He was strong.......from the inside. He'd say to Joe as a kid, "Worry? I'll tell you when to worry." Such inner power separated him from the indecisive, ineffectual crowd called men-pleasers. For that reason he had respect that cleared the charts. He was liked, admired, envied, and loved.

CHAPTER NINE

A HEART
FOR CREATIVITY

I remember wildly running into my house one day, to tell my mom that Tim McCarver just hit a homerun and that Kenny Boyer had got a hit...I split my toe open on the old time vacuum cleaner hose laying in the floor! Point being...I was THAT excited over baseball as a young child.

Nancee Cagle

Jack was emceeing an AFTRA banquet honoring St. Louisan, Yogi Berra. Jack and Yogi bantered about a special day in World War II when Yogi was on a ship firing at an incoming plane. Yogi finally shot it down. Jack said they rescued the pilot and he wasn't very happy with what had happened. He asked Yogi to explain why. "Because he was one of our men," was his sheepish response. The crowd roared with laughter.

His creativity is noted as he seemed to genuinely delight in all of us. Waiters and waitresses? Yes. Baseball buddies? Of course. Police officers? Most definitely.

One wintry night Jack left the Arena where the Blues hockey team was playing. He noticed a handful of policemen standing off in a cluster. Jack sauntered over and chatted with the guys. He stood with them for nearly a half an hour enduring the cold chill of the evening to thank them for doing a good job. Is it any wonder everyone loved Jack Buck? He gave everyone ample reason.

> *I had an elderly cousin that was a member of the Sisters of St. Joseph. She was born in 1879 and died at the age of 108. Sister was an avid St. Louis Cardinal fan, practically from the beginning of the franchise, and said many prayers for them. Jack Buck, and I believe it was Lou Brock, took time out of their busy schedules, to go to the Nazareth Retirement Home in south St. Louis County to help her celebrate her 108th birthday.*

> *Catherine Waidmann*

Reverend George Robertson tells a most touching story which is typical of sensitive-hearted Jack. A man who worked with the inner city children in Alton mentioned to George how the kids loved listening to the Cardinals and especially to Jack Buck. He said most of the kids had never left Alton nor did they have the means nor the resources to get to a Cardinal game.

George just happened to be good friends with Jack, and he told him the story of the children. Jack said, "Well we are going to do something about this. George I want you to go hire a bus and get the children to a particular game and I'll do the rest. This is your assignment". Jack gave further instructions as to where to have the bus park, where George was to park, and where to enter the stadium down below.

George obeyed orders. He made all the arrangements for the bus to deliver the kids to the stadium…just as Jack had urged. George, in turn, parked his car right where Jack had described. His Festiva fit well in the parking space between a Jag and a Porsche.

George found the children and he found Mr. Buck and got them together. Jack gave each of the kids a ticket and twenty dollars apiece. He lined them up before the players and asked all the players to give the children an autograph. One child was overheard to say, "This was the greatest day of my life!"

Toward the end, Jack was not a well man. Yet he refused to yield in those days of rugged terrain for so many needed help. Nothing seemed to keep this man from his graceful stroll. Jack returned home late one night from the game at Busch. He asked Carole if they might have any old carpet. Parkinson's made it a stretch for him to negotiate the basement stairs, yet he was successful. It was an apparent struggle for him to endure the exploration of carpet scraps. Why was he doing this? Shirley, who worked at the stadium, had trouble with her feet as the Fall temperatures made the concrete floors cold. Jack wanted to find carpet to keep her feet warmer.

To recall fond memories of this American patriot, the family patriarch, the community idol, and our friend is no stretch for any. The seedlings of Buck-isms sprouted long ago and have evolved into forests of beauty and shade for the travelers who seek refuge from the weariness of routine. Jack put life into life. He was not a self-made man. He was a self-given partner. He was never an island satisfied with the strands of life that would benefit him. He was too busy to indulge in selfishness. He had places to be, people to see, hearts to secure.

The *Voice of Silver* was God's way of letting all of us connect to this *Heart of Gold.* He reigned in sunshine. He built boats in storms. He was stronger than Rocky. He was tough in the rough times and most certain that all would be well. Jack never wavered. He was a living anchor.

KMOX,

It was spring training, 1982, Winter Haven, Florida, and the St. Louis Cardinals were visiting the Boston Red Sox that day. My friends and I spoke with Ozzie Smith, Mike Ramsey, Lonnie Smith and others, but I never stopped looking for the man with the voice of my youth. It struck me as interesting that I longed to meet a voice and not a player.

I loitered near the press box in hopes of catching a glimpse, but unfortunately I never did run into Mr. Buck. I did spot him in the small booth later from my seat as I clutched a baseball with Ozzie and Lonnie and Tommy Herr written on it, but his name never made it onto that ball. It was the one name I really wanted.

Now upon hearing of his passing, some 35 years after first hearing Jack Buck, I am surprisingly reliving many childhood memories of a Cardinal fan glued to the radio in my Southern Kentucky bedroom. I am startled at this nostalgic emotion. So much so I had to e-mail your station, something I never do. And while I realize I am in a vast number of persons that his voice touched, I had to in some small way honor his memory. Thus this mailing.

Thanks, Jack, I never knew you were so ingrained in the fabric of my childhood.

David Blankenship

April 17, 2001

Dear Jack,

Last night my husband and I arrived at the ball park and waited for the gates to open. Hank is off on Monday so it was a good night to be able to arrive in time for warm up. We enjoy being able to watch up close and all the interaction on the field.

Hank and I are partners with four other families and we share season tickets. Of course we think we have the best two seats in the ballpark, Section 246 Row 1. We enjoy sports, but baseball is our utmost favorite. Matter of fact on our first date way back in 1965 Hank took me to a Cardinals game at Sportsman Park.

A lot of "Greats" have come and gone with the Cardinal organization. All have shaped the club in some manner. But, you are still here, standing by your Cardinals, being Mr. Baseball, you are the St. Louis Cardinals, you are the "Greatest"! As far back as I can remember you have been there, the "Rock" of the Redbirds.

We in St. Louis are so fortunate to have you, a man of such great stature to represent the Cardinal organization. Well known and respected across our great country you are... like is so obvious... you down on the field last night during warm up. Everyone wants their picture taken with Jack!

You are a first class gentleman of distinction. Hank and I want to thank you for all of your dedicated years to baseball. You make us proud of our Cardinals and our city just by being you. We are so very honored and fortunate to have you, Mr. Jack Buck, the "Great" of all times in baseball.

Thank You!

Sincerely,
Hank and Lorraine Block

CHAPTER TEN

A HEART
FOR
PERSEVERANCE

I worked as an usherette at the stadium for a number of years. A few of those years I worked the Press elevator. It was also used to transport fans in wheelchairs to their section. It was inevitable that every time the elevator opened and someone in a wheelchair was waiting to get on, Mr. Buck would invite them in and tell Mattie, the elevator operator, to take them to their level first.

D. Higgins

Jack Buck knew an invaluable secret: disappointment and struggle are criteria for success. Somewhere, sometime everyone must fail. The great cellist Gaspar Cassado would tell his students, "I'm so sorry for you; your lives have been so easy. You can't play great music unless your heart's been broken.[1]" Jack could offer a healing Midas touch to a community because his heart had been broken. He knew disappointment......and the secret of what it could do "for" him.

His repertoire of talent was challenged by significant health issues. It was just like Jack to excel in every field of his life. Jack would say, "I have diabetes, a pace-maker, sciatica, cancer, vertigo, Parkinson's, eight kids and an Emmy." While poor health ran interference it was never a setback but a setforward. Everything that happened to him advantaged him....and in turn advantaged us.

> Jack knew an invaluable secret: disappointment and struggle are criteria for success.

Mr. Buck reminds me so very much of my Dad, not only in appearance but also in his generosity to his family. Mr. Buck was a part of the greatest generation, as is my almost 80 year old father, those who grew and developed their personality and depth of character through life's adversities.

Some make an impact on only their immediate family but Mr. Buck had and used the opportunities God provided through him to touch and shape many more lives.

The Schmerber Family

Someone asked him how he was doing with all the health challenges that racked his body. "I'm falling apart, but I look pretty good...don't you think?" Jack Buck successfully broke the code of a powerful secret: do not let negative things control

---

[1] **The Art of Possibility, Rosamund Stone Zander and Benjamin Zander, 31**

you, but rather learn to use them as fuel for additional personal energy. Illnesses merely gave him more material for his after-dinner speeches or one-liner wisecracks as he went through his daily routine.

He once quipped that when he and Muhammed Ali (who likewise suffered from Parkinson's) shook hands it took them thirty minutes to get the two untangled. Of course this not only gave him material for humor, it gave him a grand idea for a most unique poem.

The Club

I'm putting a social club together
with a group of my Parkinson's Pals.
It's distressing....but I have to inform you,
it's a men's club, we don't admit gals.

I doubt it will ever have a meeting,
One member doesn't live in the states.
If we do get to meet,
I know what we'll eat,
we'll have pizza and chitlins an shakes.

We have Michael J., John and Billy.
Then we have Muhammad and me.
We do have a luncheon agenda
if the time comes when everyone's free.

Mr. Graham will deliver the invocation.
Mr. Ali will do the rope-a-dope.
Mr. Fox will entertain.
I'll be the emcee
        —and our speaker will be the Pope.

How Jack could be so sly with his knack for humor in the least expecting moments. Yet, he didn't just use his gift for entertainment only. He used them for promoting good causes. Being a former smoker, consider Jack's poem written at the discovery of his own cancer.

Wake Up

I had a recent operation—
never suspected it was in the future for me—
This sort of thing happens to others
when the subject is cancer—the big C.

Every family in this country
has been affected by this dreadful condition.
Now I find I'm not one of a kind;
I'm a part of the latest edition.

I was selling papers on the corner—
15 years old—nineteen thirty-nine.
I couldn't wait to graduate, and light up
like those friends of mine.

My mother and father showed how to do it.
Old Gold was their favorite brand.
You heard a match, turned around—
they each had a cigarette in their hand.

My older brothers carried the torch,
Camels, Luckies, and Wings.
We heard no one say we'd have to pay
In more than one way for those things.

The friends I worked with at the drive-in
during the next two years
Smoked as much as I did—we were hot
A cigarette, and a couple of beers.

Then off to the Great Lakes on the ore boats
I felt like a grown up now,
sucking smoke into my lungs
as I stood at the front of the bow.

These filthy things hook and control us,
Light up first thing every day.
As we talk on the phone, when we finish a meal,
While you're driving—keep puffing away.

A cigarette and your morning coffee.
A last smoke—you turn out the light.
An early call to the bathroom,
Have a puff—make sure things feel right.

Then I joined a large group of smokers.
They gave you all the tobacco you could take.
They almost ordered you to use it
"Platoon halt! Light up—take a break."

People then learned there was a price to be paid
for the joy cigarettes were giving.
Emphysema, heart attack, cancer and stroke.
Man, this is really living.

You'd better quit before you regret it.
Have your lungs x-rayed twice a year.
Then hope they don't find any cancer—
if it's not too late, there's nothing to fear.

If they find a spot and it's early,
take a Cat Scan—hope the lymph nodes are fine
Tell your family something bad is happening,
and hope this isn't the end of the line.

In 55 years I smoked half a million
Should I have expected NOT to have cancer?

Have you had enough?
Do you need one more puff?
Wake Up!
You know the answer.

Dear Mr. Buck

First I wish to express my sympathy to the family and friends of the great Jack Buck. Like most folks in St. Louis, I feel a part of the Buck's extended family, even though I have never met any of you personally. I, too, remember listening to the Cardinals with my grandparents on a radio in their living room. That radio was bigger than some televisions are now. Jack Buck, an icon and legend, will be missed.

Second, there is a story I'd like to share with you. I teach a co-ed adult Bible Study at Maplewood Baptist Church. A few years ago, our Sunday morning lesson was focused on the joy and excitement of meeting our Savior and Lord, Jesus Christ, face to face. We were to read several passages from the Bible concerning Jesus visiting someone's house, often unexpected, and staying for a meal or overnight. The author of the material suggested asking the class how they would feel and act if a local elected official knocked on their door and asked to stay with them. I understood the point the writer was attempting to make. He was not trying to compare any of these folks with Jesus. He was trying to stir joy and honor and reverence. He was also hoping, if they imagined being in this situation, the class would say they would get on the phone and start inviting family and friends over to share in this incredible experience. However, in preparation for this lesson, I had to assess our "elected officials". I knew some of the people in my class wouldn't even know who the mayor of Maplewood was. The mayor of the City of St. Louis at the time, was very controversial and having some difficulties. And even the White House was allegedly involved in some scandalous activities. I knew this path of comparisons just was not going to achieve the deep passion, joy and enthusiasm the writer was hoping for. I could only think of one local personality who could touch those feelings. So I asked my class that Sunday, how they would feel and what would they do if they answered the doorbell and discovered Jack Buck at their door, asking them if he could stay for dinner and watch the game with them.

Oh, my! Their reaction was fabulous! They got so excited! I heard responses such as: "I'd call my parents or grandparents and tell them to get over here right away", or "I'd run up and down the street yelling", or "I'd call all my football buddies", or "I'd just stand there speechless". I knew they would share my deep feelings of respect and admiration for this very honorable man.

Jack Buck truly was a hero, our hero, … and that's a winner.

Cindy Blankenship

CHAPTER ELEVEN

A HEART
THAT SHARED

You may defer to the team as the true essence of our attraction, and that may be so, but it was you who made it live for us.

Ward Silver

300 Lobby of Busch Stadium was the entrance for this man of great character. He must have signed thousands of autographs from this location alone. He never refused anyone his celebrated signature. Toward the last days of his career, Parkinson's made this effort to be a little more of a challenge. But no, Jack saw it as one more new way to bring a smile.

Aggie Ceriotti was a long-time receptionist at this stadium post. She and Jack interacted over the years having a tremendous working relationship. As his hands trembled and his arms shook, it was more difficult to accommodate the fans with their many autograph requests. More difficult? Yes. Turn down the fans? Never! "Come on into Aggie's office," Jack would quip. "She won't mind." And as the tremors disrespected his task, he turned and said, "Aggie, why does your desk shake so much?"

I sat in the audience at a Jupiter, Florida banquet as Jack spoke. I observed his body twitch and jerk as Parkinson's made effort to master the Master. However, it could not touch his *Voice of Silver*. With arms flying and head bobbing throughout each fascinating line he shared, disease may have controlled his body, but Jack contolled the audience. He quipped, "With this Parkinson's I have to stay away from auctions. You would not believe the stuff I have bought."

At his passing, I listened to a caller from Springfield, Missouri recollect both Jack and Stan Musial's inductions into the Missouri Hall of Fame. Among the events was an auction where Jack paid $1000 for a Ken Griffey, Jr. poster. Later he was questioned as to why he would bid on something not Cardinal related. Again, he capitalized on his wit and charm. "Oh, I didn't bid on that thing. My Parkinson's did."

On another occasion Jack told Mickey Garagiola that he was at an auction and his left hand just flew up uncontrollably. He was the winning bidder and it cost him $2000. He retorted, "And Mickey, do you know what I won? An opportunity to sit in the booth with Mike Shannon and Jack Buck!"

Jack Buck fought a valiant battle against the escalating invasion of poor health. He did so with gallantry and dignity. And when did he breathe his last? Only when the Angels came to town. It was the California Angels first visit to St. Louis. When son, Joe, went on the air with KMOX to announce his father's passing, a gentle sorrow quietly settled upon St. Louis much like a snow would blanket the city.

Immediately, upon Joe's careful expression regarding his dad, callers to the station began a steady stream of public testimony giving tribute this immeasureable and irreplaceable asset to the community. Jack will always be missed and never....never forgotten. He was a grand leader because he had a servant heart. He is a touch of class.

Merely weeks after his death, the Scotland County R-1 Schools in Memphis, Missouri held their annual awards banquet, "Celebration of Excellence V". Amidst the names of important participants and their honored roles in the printed program was this quote, "People will not remember what we say or what we do. But they will always remember how we made them feel." (Jack Buck, Hall of Fame Broadcaster, St. Louis Cardinals)

The man is treasured because he is a man who was shared....by his family. Should they have been selfish, we would not have had the multi-faceted ways to connect to this hero.

To the Wonderful Buck family,

Thank you for sharing your husband, father, and friend with all of us. I am forever grateful and my deepest sympathy. I have cried many a tear. My voice of summer has moved to heaven.

His greatest gift was his ability to put a smile on our face and laughter in our heart on many a summer day.

I will dearly miss his voice—he always brought me memories of my Dad, Sportsman Park and Cardinal baseball.

Thank you for sharing!

Gayle Goedeke

Jack Buck single-handedly captured the hearts of baseball fans because he loved us first. A compliment to him is that each of us tries to find some part of ourselves that is just like him. We will desperately miss his wit and warmth.

And.........we vow to remember him.

Our brother-in-law, Randy, was diagnosed with colon cancer many years ago. My husband called Mr. Buck's office on the phone and asked if it would be possible to get tickets to a Cardinal baseball game for Randy and his family. A few evenings later, Mr. Buck called my husband at home and said, "Hi Russ, this is Jack Buck. When would Randy and his family like to go to the game?" Mr. Buck provided Randy and his family with seats right behind home plate! The evening of the game, Randy called our house from the stadium and exclaimed, "This is SO GREAT!" The joy in Randy's voice is something I will always remember. Randy, his wife and 3 sons waited outside the door to thank Mr. Buck personally for the tickets. Randy passed away months after that. This story, and countless others I have heard about Mr. Buck will always be in my memories of him. Perhaps Randy will once again shake his hand in heaven.

Emily Kuttenkuler

March 2, 2002
Dear Mr. Buck

Our 8 year old little girl has much in common with you.
Tiffany spent the first 5 months of her life in the hospital. She was born with 5 bowel obstructions and had surgery to her intestines twice with

a host of other complications during her hospital residency. At 8 years old, she has unexplained emphysema in 50% of her lungs and takes 10 doses of medication each day. In public, cigarette smoke is particularly irritating to her breathing so I am glad that you speak against it.

She is a very happy little girl who is crazy about her 4 brothers and spends most of her time hanging around high school football and baseball as my husband is coach. There's nothing that makes me more thankful and appreciative than being at a ball game with her in the fresh air. What a simple thing.

There are times that I still struggle emotionally and spiritually with her health but knowing that others are praying for her pulls me through. Please know that thousands and thousands of people are praying for your renewed strength and for the delight that each day can bring through hope.

Wishing faith, hope, & joy to you and those you love!

Stephanie Bunton

CHAPTER TWELVE

A HEART
FULL OF WINDOWS

You've obviously led by example, because your family has shown unbelievable class. You were, I'm sure, very proud to have such a wonderful family, who has been so kind to share you with all of us.

Tricia Marion

LETTERS, E-MAILS, PHOTOS

What the Cardinal world hoped would not happen, did. Jack succumbed to the multiple-health tyrants and was admitted to Barnes Jewish Hospital for his final seven months. He battled long and hard.....as did his entire family. During those long days you fans played a role you'd never have guessed. You were wonderful.

There were no windows in 2300 ICU. Your letters and notes became candles in the darkness.

Carole reminisced,

"We had such long, long days in ICU. Every ray of hope came from your letters and notes. It was important that they be written."

She saved all the letters. Your words...your abundantly kind hearts kept the family in touch with St. Louis and her surroundings. Here is a collection of letters, e-mails, and pictures that we have chosen.

Carole Buck

Jack,

My fondest memories are anchored with your distinctive and reassuring voice. While we have never met, I feel so close to you, and you have been in my prayers since learning of your setback. Whether it was Christmas morning when you brought my family into your home, or insomnia during a late night Cardinal game that went well past my bed-time, your voice has always comforted me.

I hope my words of gratitude, with all of the others, are of some comfort to you.

Karl Krummenacher

— — — — — — — — — — — — — — — — — —

Dear Mr. Buck,

This city loves you and misses you. No matter what the future holds for you I wish you health and happiness and whatever your heart desires.

Angel

— — — — — — — — — — — — — — — — — —

To a dear man: You may not know me, you may not know the many people sending messages, but we love you and pray you will soon feel better.

Linda L.

— — — — — — — — — — — — — — — — — —

Dear Jack,
I want to wish you a speedy recovery and best wishes from Storm Lake, Iowa. I became a Cardinal and Jack Buck fan because our radio station KAYL used to carry the Cards back in the '70's.

Best wishes,
Steve Berg

June 21, 2002

Dear Mrs. Buck and Family,

I have thrown batting practice for the Cardinals for fifteen years. That means I have known Mr. Buck for fifteen years as well. As the years went by, I got to know him better, especially when he and my pastor, Rodney, got to be close friends. Every Sunday game that I missed church to throw batting practice, Mr. Buck would always tell me he was going to tell Rodney. One Sunday he said he caught me looking in the stands at a pretty girl and he was making sure Rodney knew what I was doing!

My greatest regret is that I didn't have tapes made of the three interviews I had with Mr. Buck. My first was in Chicago, my first road trip with the club. I was so nervous…here I was getting interviewed by a legend. But by the time the interview started, Mr. Buck had put me completely at ease. His manner of interviewing made it so easy.

One day shortly after his book came out, I asked him if I got one, if he would mind signing it for me. He told me to go to Sam's Club, that they were cheaper there. We laughed, but the very next day I was in our locker room , stuck way in the back of nowhere, and here came Mr. Buck with one of his books signed to me. The first thing that came to my mind was, he went to Sam's himself? Knowing this wouldn't be the case, I also knew that he would have done so if he had to. But at the time I was amazed first, that he remembered and second, that he took the time to go out of his way to give me the book personally. But now, I am not amazed. I came to know that was the way Mr. Buck was. To be honest, we BP pitchers are sort of the forgotten few, but Mr. Buck always treated us like we were his friend, because we were.

Many have said it is an honor to have known Mr. Buck, and it most certainly is. But to me the honor is that Mr. Buck knew me, that he knew my name and that I was his friend. I will forever miss him. My family and I will keep all of you in our prayers.

With deepest sympathy,
John Lackey

July 11,2002

The Legend of Jack Buck with a Personal Touch

This is one column I don't want to write. But I have to honor a man who put joy into life. For so many, Jack Buck was larger than life. He was celebrity and baseball royalty, all rolled into one. For me, he was someone who never acted like it.

When I started working at KMOX seven years ago, I knew what a well-known broadcaster he was, but I didn't know what a charitable man he was. I didn't know that he made the people who cleaned the building the part-timers and the interns feel that he was interested in them. I didn't know that he handed out $100.00 bills to the hourly employees and refused to take them back. I didn't know that he was such a great poet and story teller.

Once on the air, I told him I had to MC an event that night and I needed some advice. He told me that when I step up to the podium tell the audience, I'm not here to bore you, but I am here to introduce the people that will.

Jack Buck lived a full life. I will never forget a story he told on the air. He came into the studio for his biweekly discussion with us during afternoon drive. When I introduced Jack on the air, he said, Guess what I did today? Now because his social circle included other Hall of Famers, and actors and politicians, I thought he might tell a funny story about meeting up with one of them.

I jumped out of a perfectly good airplane today, Buck said.

Jack, you mean you went skydiving?

Yes I did.

I had to ask him then, Does Carole know? And Jack Buck replied, She does now.

Although he had been a broadcaster for the Cardinals for nearly 50 years, our conversations with him weren't only about baseball. Once, we were in the middle of our segment and I heard a commotion in the background. Now, I knew Jack was at home and I asked him if everything was okay. He said he was baby-sitting one of his grandchildren and she'd just broken a lamp. Without skipping a beat, he said, I don't think they'll let me baby-sit anymore.

One of the things I will miss most about Jack Buck is hearing his poetry and watching him stroll into the newsroom and start singing to me. If I knew the words, I would try to harmonize. If I didn't have a clue, I would just hum along.

There were also times he would debut poems on the air, like the one about the club he said he recently joined. It was about Parkinson's disease.

He would bring some of his poems into the station, freshly handwritten on a yellow legal pad and he would read them to me. Once he asked me to read one of his new creations out loud. Of course, I did, but talk about being nervous.

Jack Buck is gone now, but his legacy is strong through his charitable work and his greatest pride and joy, his family. I just wish I had been able to see him one more time to tell him how special I thought he was.

Carol Daniel

Jack Buck with Carol Daniel

To Jack Buck's Family,
    Our deepest sympathy
to all of you.
    We are not important
people or have any money
but we are Cardinal Fans
for over fifty years.
    Our thoughts and
prayers are with you all.
    Did not know your Dad
but felt like we did.

            Cardinal Fans forever
         Bob & Geneva Krouse &
                    Family -
         2901 So. 14
         Springfield.
            Illinois

I wish to send my best wishes to Mr. Jack Buck. I have been a longtime die-hard fan of the St. Louis Cardinals since the early 60's. It's been hard to listen to the games on KMOX without Mr. Buck broadcasting the games even though Mike Shannon has done a tremendous job. I grew up in St. Louis and now reside in Nashville, TN., and drive a semi for a living, so I get to listen to most of your ballgames on KMOX. Wish Mr. Jack Buck a speedy recovery and hope to hear his knowledgeable insight on the St. Louis Cardinals' radio network soon.

Lee "Wrongway" Starr

— — — — — — — — — — — — — — — — — — — —

Mr. Buck,
My husband, aunt, and I listen to the Cardinal games every night here in Memphis. We have missed your wonderful voice and special commentary so much! You're the best!

Julie and Gary Sims
Martha Barbee

— — — — — — — — — — — — — — — — — — — —

Jack—We love you and miss you. Our prayers are with you. Get well soon.

Charlie and Jan Sadler

— — — — — — — — — — — — — — — — — — — —

Jack,
I hope you feel better soon. I enjoyed very much working with you at NBC doing the "color" to your brilliant play by play. You were a pro's pro and a class act and I consider you a mentor. Thank you and best wishes,

Andy Russell

— — — — — — — — — — — — — — — — — — — —

Dear Jack,
I hope that you are feeling better! I can't wait until you're back in the booth. I hope that you are announcing the World Series games when the Cardinals make it. I'm looking forward to when you return to broadcasting and GET WELL SOON!

Lyle Whitworth

Christine:

It's been 22 years... but I think you'll remember me because I was the first one to point out to you that "Love Stinks".

I'm so sorry for the loss of your dad. My first exposure to his talent came in 1969 when I was 14 and began my radio career riding 'gain' on the Cardinal games at their affiliate in Kennett, my hometown, down in the boot heel. Every inning and a half the 'local' break came. Turn down the knob. Turn up this knob and push the button to play the local spot. It was exciting for a 14-year old. Even more so to listen in on 'cue' as Jack or Harry cleared their throat and exchanged a word or two as they prepared for air. Then a 'professional' voice would say: "This is KMOX in St. Louis. Skies are clear. We're going to play a baseball game today at 1:05. We're 5 minutes from the start. Here's your timecheck. At the mark, it will be exactly 1:00 PM Central Daylight Time.........wolf!" (Never did understand why that guy said "wolf".)

Every half-hour I got to open the mike after your dad said: "This is St. Louis Cardinals Baseball Network... and then went quiet for 10, seconds, crowd noise only, as I crammed as much information into 10 seconds as was humanly possible; "This is KBOA FM in Kennett, Missouri. 85 degrees at 4:30. The forecast calls for partly cloudy skies today with an 80% chance of scattered afternoon showers. Stay tuned after the game for Platter Party!"

West coast, extra-inning games that began at 10 PM were a killer for a high-school student who walked 1-mile home across the cotton fields at 2:30 AM. Only prayed Gibson was pitching because he didn't waste time worrying about the hitter.

What a thrill it was years later to meet Jack Buck – in that very pressbox. You were my excuse, my courage to walk up and introduce myself to your dad – "Hi, Mr. Buck, I work with Christine at KPLR. I'm the weekend sports guy. My name is Jeff." He was a real gentleman to me. Introduced me to Roger Maris who just happened to be there and I didn't even recognize. Was more thrilled to meet your Dad than sad Roger.

He was the best, Chris. The best there ever was. My deepest sympathy to you and your family.

Jeff Pylant

WILLIAM J. CLINTON
6-20-02

Dear Joe —
    I was so sorry to hear of your father's death. Growing up in Arkansas in the 50s, the Cardinals were my team. I did my homework in grade school listening to your dad call the Cardinals games on radio. He left me and countless others with great memories.
                    Sincerely
                    Bill Clinton

Bill Clinton -Former President

Dear Joe,

    My deepest sympathy to you and your family. Jack was special to all of us. You are special, too, and I admire you as a personal and as a professional. All my best -

                                Ernie Hamwel

In the mid eighties, My younger girlfriend and I were walking out of the stadium when we saw Jack Buck.

I was thrilled as we walked side by side and a simple conversation began. I took a moment to introduce Jack to the naive female who had accompanied me. "This is Jack Buck."

Dumbfounded, she replied, " o?!"

I was embarrassed, until he took the matter into his own hands and quipped, "What's your name young lady?"

She chimed, "I'm Kris from Waterloo!"

Then, with a shake of his head, and in such an endearing light, he replied, "So?!"

My brush with greatness. Thank you Mr. Buck for that and so many memories. Get well soon!

Mike Robertson

Dear Carole,

Enclosed is a picture of my son Chris (who was 12 at the time) with Jack taken at Spring Training at Al Lang Field 3/19/93.

Because I had a telephoto lens I had to keep backing up to get this shot. Jack was very patient, even though the game was about to start and he was running late to the broadcast booth. He said, " Ok how's this?" As you can see, it was rather windy. In any case, it was the first time I met Jack and was so impressed on how he handled the barrage of fans seeking pictures or autographs.

Sincerely,
Philip B. Cady, Sr. "Flip"

Dear Carol:

Better writers than I have written tributes to and memories of Jack over the last week. And we have enjoyed reading them all. We are overwhelmed, but not, amazed by how many of us Jack touched, how many of us feel his loss so keenly. The sheer numbers who count ourselves among Jack's friend must set a record.

I consider our family one of the very fortunate ones. Our memories with Jack go back almost fifty years. How fortunate I was to have Jack emcee the special dinners, which meant so much to me and my family, especially the first Cystic Fibrosis roast, a cause which owes so much to Jack's interest and time. Martha and I have been talking about the trip we took together with the Roarty's and what a great time we all had.

I also want to share with you the many unselfish, caring and very generous moments, which we treasured with Jack at Tony's. In his own inimitable style, Jack always took the time when he visited here to chat with the staff. Among the thousands of celebrities we have welcomed, none have been as gracious with our staff as Jack. Throughout Tony's , our staff are telling, " Jack stories," and we are laughing again. As large as he was, he made time for everyone. What a gift he had, what a gift he gave each of us.

Jack was the most gracious man I ever met, and this grace is apparent in the book of poems he wrote. I gave this book to the members of my family, a real keepsake for all of us. We will think of Jack often, as we share a memory and retell a joke, of course, not as well as he did. And, I will give more of myself as he taught us all to do.

Vincent J. Bommarito

Ron,

I don't know if I'm sending this to make you and the KMOX family feel better or just to express my feelings on the passing of Jack Buck.

Typically when someone passes it is easy for his or her close friends and relatives to relay their feelings on the individual in a personal tribute.

I have been listening to the station all morning and through all the interviews with Mike Roarty, Tommy LaSorda, Jerry Clinton and the others there is one common theme. No one has been able to articulate with any brevity the life of Jack Buck and what he meant to them, baseball, the city, and everyone.

These are people who have spent their lives speaking and communicating as their business. When the best communicators, coaches, business people and salesmen can't sum up the lifelong contributions of one man, then the true extent of the loss can never be measured or understood. Consequently, the positive influence and contributions Jack Buck made to the quality of life on this planet is immeasurable.

I'll bet a case of Budweiser and a dozen Big Macs that every individual within 120 miles of the arch has a memory of Jack Buck they can easily recall. That's a legacy.

Take care.

Mr. Jack Buck   May 23, 2001
St. Louis Cardinals

Dear Jack:

It's been a while since I have heard you do Cardinals games; guess I haven't been "paying attention" re your malady, but Rick Reilly's article in *SI* woke me up…

I, along with legions of others, want to congratulate you on a spectacular career and let you know how important your voice was to a kid, now an old man, who grew up in Webster Groves and worshipped the Cardinals… bike to the Clayton Courthouse at 10:00 am on Sunday, take the Redbird Express to Sportsman's Park, Grand and Dodier, watch BP, watch both ends of the double header, back on the Redbird Express, bike from Clayton to Webster, home by midnight… or riding with my grandfather every other week end to the farms in Sikeston… never miss a game… Jabo and Rip and Bill (Virdon, never a Pirate to me) and Kenny and Marty (at the end) and Wally (Moon, never a Dodger to me) and Vinegar and Gene Greene and Tom Alston, and Blazer and Red and Gibby and Bill (White) and, oh yeah, Da Man. And I have the sense that every one of these wonderful memories were always "brought to you (me) by Jack Buck." Your voice was the music bed for the game/song. Your wit and imagination were the fabric that always pushed this boring "past time" to the front edge of my psyche… and kept it there.

As far as this kid form Webster Groves knows, no Cardinal game has ever started or will ever start without the voice of Jack Buck… Parkinson's Disease or not.

                                                      Regards,

                                                      Kit Mill

Dear Carole and Family,

I am deeply sorrowful that I cannot be with you to share your grief as well as celebrate the life of my friend, Mr. Buck. I have responsibilities at our national church assembly that providentially prevent me from being with you today. Though I tried to make it work even by means of private plane, in the end I could not. Thank you for being so understanding.

You have given me the privilege of sharing many special moments with you as a family. We have shared Christmases together during the annual radio broadcast and we have worshipped together. I have important memories with some of you as individuals. I will forever cherish our lunch, Joe, in which you shared the profound impact your father has had on your life and profession. Julie and Jeff, we shared some great moments together during pre-marriage counseling. Thank you for the high privilege of letting me officiate your wedding. It was a momentous occasion for many reasons, not the least of which was that your father managed to give you away while never missing a beat with his chewing gum! And Beverly and Bonnie, it was a deeply moving experience to watch your tender care of your father that one afternoon you graciously allowed me to visit your father.

Mr. Buck was a good friend to me. He graciously listened to the sermons of a young preacher and offered regular encouragement. And in private times we shared conversations of deep spiritual significance. He did have many friends in high places, but he was also a friend to little people like me and many, many others. That friendship flowed out of his theology, which I related on the day we dedicated the statue at Busch Stadium. Carole, I know you asked him many times what he would say to God when God asked him why he should let Mr. Buck into heaven. The answer he recorded in his book was not a statement but a question, "Lord, why have you been so good to me?"

Certainly he knew that no one deserves the goodness of God. We are all sinners and estranged from him. But the Good News of the Gospel is that at the right moment God demonstrated his love by sending his Son to die for those who would receive him as Lord and Savior. Those who ask Christ to apply that Gospel to them are forgiven all of their sins. Now that's a winner of a Gospel! It was my privilege to celebrate this Good News with Mr. Buck while praying with him a few weeks ago. And I know that many of you are celebrating the comfort of that same Gospel today in your grief.

Again, I am sorry that I cannot be with you, but I assure you of my prayers and my love. I will certainly check on you when I return.

May the love of Christ be with you all and thank you for your friendship.

Love,
George Robertson

.....Living in Hannibal, the daughter of a dairy farmer who only got interested in baseball when the playoffs started, I have no opportunity to go to Busch Stadium to watch the Cardinals play. Jack was my eyes and my ticket to the game for many years before I was finally able to come to Busch Stadium as a teenager and see first hand what Jack had been telling me about for years....

Judge Mary Russell

- -

Dear Jack,
Though we never met, you are a friend. All those years painting word pictures so we could understand.....thanks! We want you back but don't hurry—let the young "bucks" do the heavy lifting. You are in our prayers.

Sincerely,
LeRoy and Robeta Knox

- -

Jack,

Sorry to read you have not been feeling too well. Sure hope things move along for speedy recovery. Things would never be the same without you in the booth. Take care—I'll be listening. I get KMOX loud and clear here in Northern Michigan in the evening.

Tony McCleery

You are in our thoughts and prayers.
We Miss You!

Brendan   Moriah

Amy   Laura   gnilu

Your Friends at
St. Joseph Institute for the Deaf

Brook   Megan   Hilary   Nate   Austin
LUZ

So Long For Just A While, Mr. Buck

Dustin McKinnis a 2002 graduate of Central High School, met Jack Buck in 1995 and occasionally shared the Cardinals broadcast booth with him. McKinnis has had more than 100 operations to repair problems related to his tracheal tube.

By Dustin McKinnis

That's a winner! Those famous words describe Jack Buck in everthing he did. Not only was he an outstanding and gifted announcer, but he was an even better person.

Jack Buck gave his all to his family, his friends, his broadcasts and the fans. No matter what team you were cheering for one could equally cheer for Jack Buck as well. His incredible knowledge and love for the game were evident with every word he spoke.

I had the privilege to become a very close friend of Mr. Buck and his family. I met Mr. Buck in the summer of 1995 when a friend who works at Busch Stadium introduced us. Mr. Buck and I instantly began a lasting friendship. From the moment I met him I knew how spectacular a man he was. After talking for a while, he invited my family and me to be in the broadcast booth to watch the game between the Cardinals and Reds.

Mr. Buck soon took me under his wing. He invited me to the microphone to interview me on the air. He wanted to talk to me about the 89 operations I had up to that point. He told me I was a true fighter.

Before the interview was over, Mr. Buck said he wanted me to try play-by-play. I was honored to share the microphone with a man I respected and looked up to for so many years. I called the final out in the third inning. It was a great thrill. We kept in close contact following that season.

The following season, while I was visiting Mr. Buck in the booth, he said he wanted me to do some more play-by -play. This time he told me, " I want you to yell, "That's a winner!" When I heard him say that my mouth dropped. I actually couldn't believe Mr. Buck wanted me to use his signature line.

There were two outs, and he turned the microphone over to me. Cincinnati ended up getting two hits. I vividly remember what Mr. Buck turned to me and said: " Kid, I'm going to blow you out of that chair if you don't get this next guy out." A ground ball was hit to second and thrown to first for the victory, and I yelled his famous line. I remember Mr. Buck having tears building in his eyes and a big smile on his face. It not only meant a lot to me, but to him as well.

Unforgettable Moments

Those experiences are moments I will never forget and will always treasure. I witnessed the special side of Jack Buck, who showed me his tender heart. He was concerned and thought of others before himself.

I have been fortunate to have many great experiences and memories with Mr.. Buck. A few that stand out most in my mind are being next to Mr. Buck when Mark McGwire hit his 62nd home run to break Roger Maris' record; being with the Buck family as they unveiled his bust outside Busch Stadium, when I discovered that Mr. Buck had written about our relationship in his autobiography; and the time Mr. Buck came to my house to visit me following one of my surgeries.

The greatest experience, though, is being able to call the Buck family my friends. No matter if it was phone calls or visits, Mr. Buck had a huge and indescribable impact on my life.

During the services Thursday, I was able to laugh and cry again with Mr. Buck. It was touching. Mr. Buck had endless great qualities, but the best was his generous heart. I hope some day I can be like Jack Buck, an honest, caring, generous, loving man who always put others before him. The gift of the friendship Mr. Buck gave me will be treasured forever and never forgotten. I will dearly miss him.

Mrs. Buck asked her husband a while back what he was going to ask the Lord when his time on earth was done. Mr. Buck replied in his humble way, " Why have you been so good to me?" I know without a doubt what the Lord's answer was at 11:08 P.M. Tuesday when Mr. Buck passed away. The Lord most likely responded, " Because you're a winner!"

As I close, I would like to steal a line from a precious friend.

So long for just a while.

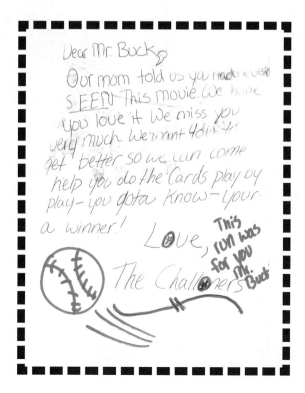

91

Dear Carole..... We had just watched the game from the bleachers. I couldn't afford expensive seats ...Anyway, I mentioned to the girls that we ought to go see Jack Buck after the game. They said " But Dad, We can't go up there' I said " Well lets go see if we can just see him and say Hi". We waited for him to show up after all of the post-game updates and I greeted him from behind the ropes. He said " Come on in." I couldn't believe it at first, but we came on in. He gave us the VIP treatment...

Paul Wood

Mindy Wood, Jack Buck,
Kelly Gafney

Clayton Book Store
Paul Wood, Jack Buck

We will miss you Jack, but at least you have left the pain behind. I'd give anything to hear you call one more game, one more inning, one more out, one more pitch. You brought the Cardinals to me through my static filled radio in KC many, many nights. You were St. Louis Cardinals baseball, and we won't forget that. Heaven got a good one today, "That's a win-ner!"

Rob Shoemaker, lifelong Cards fan

Jack Buck was at the top of the list of nice people I have had the pleasure of knowing in more than 30 years in the Communication profession. Jack was genuine. He never let his wealth of talents overshadow his humanity. His "common folks" style and demeanor endeared him to countless thousands. Jack WAS what his public persona suggested... a really nice guy.

I was about 24 when I met Jack Buck in 1972 in press row at Busch Stadium during a Cards/Cubs game. He was talking to some notable people when he spotted me, standing alone about 20 feet away. He walked over and introduced himself. He was very interested in my career aspirations. He was sincerely interested in what I had going on and what plans I had for the future.

Years later when I got on KMOX, Jack treated me with respect and dignity. Even though he had no equal in the business, he always regarded me and other KMOX staff as colleagues.

His broadcasting accomplishments, great that they are, pale in comparison to the personal attributes that made Jack Buck truly a giant of a man.

Tom Dehner
WSIE Radio (KMOX News – 1979-80, 1991-94)

I've always associated Jack Buck with my memories of my own grandfather, who, like Jack, was a dedicated family man. At my grandfather's funeral, I gave a eulogy that ended with some sentiments about what I felt I had inherited from him: a sense of decency, a love for God & family, and a strong value system. I'm feeling the same way today about Jack Buck- like I've just inherited a fortune...like I'm an heir to something so much more precious and dear than money or possessions. Jack Buck left behind a great legacy...and we are ALL his heirs.

Brenda Ruzicka

To All The Buck Family-

My extreme sympathy for your loss and the biggest loss to Professional Broadcast History!

I am aware that with the deluge of cards and mail, there is little chance that you will have the opportunity to read this, but if you do, here are my thoughts- I am 58 years old and I'm sitting here crying like a baby! The loss of Jack goes so far beyond your family – it's hard to imagine! Having been born and raised in St. Louis, I spent my life there until I moved to Lake of the Ozarks in 1989 to start a business.

From the time I was born (the "Radio" says) I can remember my mother – an avid cardinal baseball fan – listening to every game on the old Westinghouse tube console radio in our family room. In the early days it was Harry Caray, but my most memorable moments were those of Jack Buck – The Voice of the Cardinals! Anytime I heard his voice it brought back those wonderful memories of my youth and the excitement of the family as he so aptly brought the play by play to our homes. When I moved to Lake of the Ozarks, I knew I could count on Jack's familiar voice to make me feel close to home.

I had the honor to meet Jack while employed at Busch Stadium as a technician in the Sports Hall of Fame in 1967-1968. He was a wonderful person who would stop and say hi to all who crossed his path. I was also privileged to meet him again at the Missouri Sports Hall of Fame inductions which he hosted several years ago.

I will miss him greatly, but what a wonderful job Joe is doing as His successor. Joe's voice is now my link to St. Louis.

Again, My deepest sympathy, Larry Brieserusto

Carole

I've delayed writing this, because I wasn't sure you'd remember me. I was the PR director of The Muny in the 1980's, and you and I worked on several projects, notably the salute to the Broadway cast of "Gigi" when it came to town.

I am also a younger brother of the Benchwarmer, the late Bob Burnes, who, as you know, was a dear friend of Jack's. When Bob's daughter, Cathy, the sportswriter, died so young, Bob told me Jack was the first one at the funeral home, and he stayed all day. "He could make two or three of these a day, seven days a week, if he wanted to, but he stayed all day with Adele and me." Bob told me. And then when Bob died, it was the same story...

Regrettably, I wasn't associated that often with jack, but whenever we were, he was always so gracious. I was the family representative on the one-hour special on the Benchwarmer that Jack hosted on KMOX Radio, and it will remain very special for me.

As spokesman for the U.S. 4th Army's Reunion Band, which was holding forth in Houston last week, I chose Jack's poem after 9/11 to read.

My wife was the co-owner of a family business on St. Louis' near north side, and she always remarked about Jack's regular visits at Thanksgiving at Holy Trinity church for the police and northside businessmen's benefit for the poor. With that in mind, we are making a contribution to the Backstoppers in his name.

I've heard so often in the last week or so, the story that if Jack met God, he'd ask "Why have you been so good to me?" I find that question easy to answer: he did what God wants us all to do – enjoy life, and along the way, reach out and help those less fortunate. Jack did that by the bushel basket full.

For St. Louis, there may be founders, mayors, even Charley Lindburghs, but based on what I saw last week, Jack Buck, and his wonderful family, are St. Louis. No contest.

Maybe we'll run into you at The Muny. After all, "How to Succeed in Business..." is up next.

God Bless.
Don Burnes.

This letter was sent to Jack in Braille:

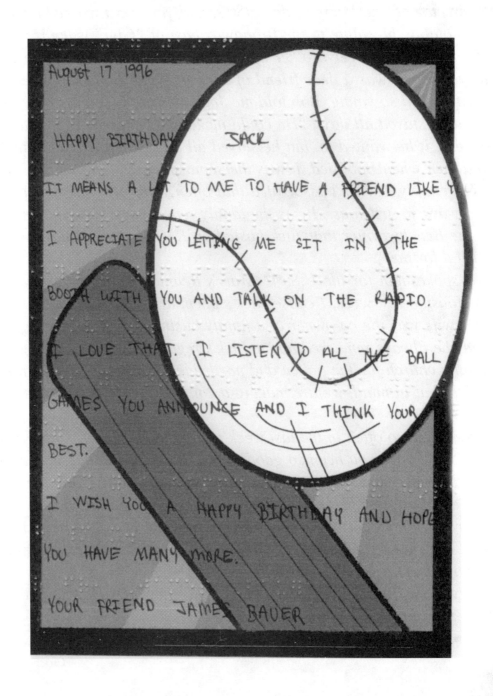

August 17 1996

HAPPY BIRTHDAY JACK

IT MEANS A LOT TO ME TO HAVE A FRIEND LIKE Y

I APPRECIATE YOU LETTING ME SIT IN THE

BOOTH WITH YOU AND TALK ON THE RADIO.

I LOVE THAT. I LISTEN TO ALL THE BALL

GAMES YOU ANNOUNCE AND I THINK YOUR

BEST.

I WISH YOU A HAPPY BIRTHDAY AND HOPE

YOU HAVE MANY MORE.

YOUR FRIEND JAMES BAUER

To Whom It May Concern:

I am writing to express my sincere sympathy on the loss of one of the greatest broadcasters of all time. More importantly, the world has lost a terrific human being. In his memory, I have composed a poem, my very first, and friends tell me I should send it along to you. I hope I have done Mr. Buck service, as I feel I had his spirit with me when I wrote it.

A Tribute to Jack

Cardinal radio broadcasts will never be the same,
Because Jack Buck is now in Heaven's Hall of Fame.
Jack, you made the game come alive with your calls-
Home runs, stolen bases, strikes and balls.

In the booth with Mike and son Joe at your side,
Your listeners navigated the game with you as our guide.
Big Mac's awesome swing, Lou's speedy legs, Gibby's fierce arm,
You described them all to us with eloquence and charm.

Your voice soothed and excited on those warm summer nights,
And your smile shown brighter than a tier of stadium lights.
The poem you wrote on that dark September day
Gave us such strength and took our fears away.

You were loved by the fans, their announcer of choice.
Even though you are gone, we can still hear your voice
In the crack of the bat and the roar of the crowd;
The way you loved the Cardinals made us all proud.

As we watch the fans file past you in an orderly line,
And we see you leave Busch Stadium for the very last time,
We remember you fondly with a tear in our eye.
So long for just a while, Jack, Godspeed and good-bye.

Daniel Kinzel

Jack was, the voice, the heart, and the soul of the city.

"It looks just like me."

June 25, 2001

To Mrs. Jack Buck and the entire Buck family;

I wanted to express my condolences on the death of Mr. Jack Buck. He was an icon in the sports community and St. Louis baseball. But equally as important, and as has been attested by many other individuals, he was friendly to everyone he encountered. All of us are richer for having had a brief experience with him.

My personal story involves my father, now 80 years old and home bound. My dad, Clay Kerley, played baseball for years, with the Union Printers, the National Association of Professional Baseball League, and would have eventually been signed by the Browns, had he not entered the Armed Services in December 1942. He also played in the Signal Corps Baseball League and qualified for the All Stars team. He made quite a name for himself and was inducted into the Amateur Hall of Fame in 1986.

It was our thrill in the late '60's, for my sisters and I to earn the straight "A" tickets from the Cardinals for our high school grades, and treat our dad to the Cardinal baseball games. For all other games, we would listen to them on the radio and grew up appreciating the game through Jack Buck's calls.

For Father's Day five years ago, I bought my dad Mr. Buck's book, "That's a Winner" and we brought it with us to a night game in the hopes of getting it autographed. The game ran into extra innings and it was almost midnight before Mr. Buck emerged form the office doors where we were waiting. The long night and severe heat had obviously taking its toll on Mr. Buck, but when my dad called out to him, Mr. Buck stopped long enough for my dad to ask for his autograph and for my sister to get a photo of the two of them.

It was a highlight for my dad and also for my twin sons and two nephews to witness that special moment. My dad will probably always wonder what would have happened had he pursued his baseball career, but he created a wonderful memory book for each of his children, with all of his baseball newspaper clippings, photos, and rankings, etc. The last page of his scrapbook contains the photo of him and Mr. Buck taken that night. We will always cherish that photo and thank Mr. Buck for being so kind and gracious to him that night. It was the last ballgame that my dad was able to attend.

I remember more recently, last year, when Mr. Buck honored our Boeing veterans at a special ceremony on our headquarter campus. He read the famous poem that he composed following the 9/11 tragedy. While walking from the building to the stage, his condition appeared fragile, but his presence and poise and character were never more strong than when he delivered the poem, accompanied to music, and additional remarks to all of our employees and veterans. I will forever be grateful that I was witness to such a great man and humanitarian.

Mr. Jack Buck will hold a place in history, that is for sure, but he will hold a special place in all of our hearts as well – those of us he touched for a mere brief moment, but a moment that will forever be burned in our memory and in our heart.

Thank you for being such a wonderfully open family to all of us who dearly loved Mr. Buck and everything he stood for. Thank you for sharing him with all of us. You are a remarkable family.

Sincerely,
Bonnie Brandt

--- --- --- --- --- --- --- --- --- --- ---

Jack,
I miss hearing your voice on the radio. You are a man who is loved by so many— what an honor. You are in my thoughts and prayers.

God bless you and your family,
Mrs. Darlene Engel

--- --- --- --- --- --- --- --- --- --- ---

Dear Jack,
It sounds to me as if you went in for a tune-up and wound up being given a total re-tooling job. I'll bet you're good for at least another million miles! But tell your doctors they've enjoyed more than their share of your wonderful wit. We need you back on the air! Thinking of you everyday—

Cheers—
Betsy Bruce

Dear Mr. Buck,

Throughout the years, I have enjoyed listening to you, as so many of us have. It wasn't until recently that I truly realized how much of an honor and privilege it is to have YOU as OUR sports voice of the St. Louis Cardinals.

I had not spoken to my dad for many years. When I was about 9, he and my mother were divorced, and I really haven't had any contact with him since he moved to California. A couple of months ago I decided to try to contact him. I finally got the nerve to call him, and when he answered it was a bit awkward, to say the least. That is, until we started talking about baseball. He told me a story that made me feel like a school kid again (I'm 37 now). In 1971, we moved from Atlanta, GA to Florissant, MO. As the story goes, my dad wasn't a baseball fan, at all. He was doing some work on the house, and had the radio tuned to KMOX, just because there " wasn't much else on." Time went by, and you can guess the outcome. Sure enough, a Cardinal's game was on, and as the weekend came and went, he said those two baseball games being broadcast by you, Mr. Buck, made him into a St. Louis Cardinal's baseball fan. As he put it, he could "see what was happening on the field." He now lives in California, and says he misses listening to those games being broadcast by you.

Mr. Buck, I wanted to write this letter back then, and I apologize that I didn't. You will probably never know the impact that you have had on so many individuals throughout the country. I am sure there are many stories like this that remain untold. I don't know if you will ever read this letter. But if you do, I hope that it makes you feel special, because you really are a special person, and a wonderful broadcaster.

Thank you for all the wonderful memories that you have given us. Our thoughts and prayers are with you and your family. Get well soon!

Best Wishes,
Clay Mun

Jack Buck
(1924-2002)

I WOKE UP THIS MORNING, TURNED ON THE TV
NOT KNOWING WHAT NEWS, WAS WAITING FOR ME

IT SEEMS OVERNIGHT, WE LOST A GREAT MAN
A HERO TO MANY, JACK BUCK, A LEGEND

IT'S HARD TO IMAGINE, THAT HE'S REALLY GONE
HE'S ACCOMPLISHED SO MUCH, BUT HIS WORK HERE IS DONE

SO MANY MEMORIES, HE LEFT IN HIS WAKE
THE VOICE OF THE CARDINALS, NOW THAT VOICE MAKES US ACHE

I GREW UP WITH THE CARDINALS, JACK BUCK, HARRY CARAY
NOW WITH BOTH OF THEM GONE, THE OUTLOOK SEEMS SCARY

JACK BUCK HAD A GIFT, TO PAINT PICTURES WITH WORDS
HIS EXCITEMENT SHOWED THROUGH, WITH HIS VOICE THAT WE HEARD

TO ST LOUIS, A LEGEND , TO HIS FANS, HE'S A TREASURE
TO HEAR JACK BUCK SPEAK, WAS TRULY A PLEASURE

TO OLD BASEBALL FANS OR EVEN BEGINNERS
OUR PULSES WOULD RACE, WHEN WE HEARD "THAT'S A WINNER!"

"GO CRAZY, FOLKS! GO CRAZY!" WAS HIS PERSONAL, CHANT
IMAGINE NOT HEARING THAT YELL, NO I CAN'T

I HOPE THAT HE KNEW, WHAT HE MEANT TO US ALL
HIS NAME GAVE NEW MEANING TO THE GAME OF BASEBALL

HE TOUCHED MANY LIVES, WITH CARING AND LOVE
WE PRAY FOR SAFE JOURNEY, TO GOD UP ABOVE

BY PAT BARNETT

Jack,

The sun always shines when you're around! Get well soon, we miss you. A listener of yours since you came to St. Louis. I can't wait to hear you again. I am 81 years old...followed the Cardinals since France Laux days.

Love,
Jim Gibbs

— — — — — — — — — — — — — — — — — — —

To a friend of every St. Louisan...we all hope for a wonderful recovery. We all desperately miss you, Jack.....you are the Best! The icing on the cake! Everyone knows your slogans...they are known country-wide! I know other cities would love to have someone like you...a hero.

Melissa Lewis

— — — — — — — — — — — — — — — — — — —

Dear Jack,
Thank you for being a "Rainbow" to us all. You've touched our lives in so many ways—all for the better! I consider myself both blessed and lucky to be in your audience.

Frank P. Uhlenbrock

— — — — — — — — — — — — — — — — — — —

Dear Carole:
You don't need me to tell you what a terrific person Jack was, but I feel compelled to do so because it is the truth. With the proper climate and late at night, we could pick up KMOX here in Ohio. It was treat for me to one-day meet Jack and then to be able to call him a friend—that was really special!

John Bankert

Uncle Joe recalls special times

Joe Arndt sat at his Formica kitchen table Thursday watching the memorial tribute to Jack Buck on a small television perched above the refrigerator of his Clayton home. Minor injuries and stiff joints from a nasty tumble last week prevented him from attending the event at Busch stadium.

Many people felt as if Buck was their best friend. Arndt, 82, really was an intimate friend of Buck's.

The Bucks refer to Arndt as their "Uncle Joe." Wearing a pressed pink shirt, dark slacks and a leather belt, Arndt watched the television intently as Buck's friends and family took to the podium to tell stories of the legendary radio announcer. "Everyone remembers Jack for his broadcasting," Arndt said. "But most importantly, he was a nice person. He was very generous with his time and money. No matter how busy he was, he'd stop to sign an autograph. People always came before the job." Arndt met Buck in the early '60's at a bar in Clayton called The Boardroom, which has since closed. The two played blackjack with several other men in a back room. "All I remember from those days was that Jack was always a lot of fun, "Arndt said.

A lifetime friendship ensued. Arndt is the godfather of Buck's daughter Julie and is considered part of the Buck family.

For almost three decades, Arndt hosted a gentlemen's poker game in his dining room on Monday nights. Those in attendance included, among others, football great Dan Dierdorf, Yankees manager Joe Torre and , of course, Jack Buck.

"The only time I ever saw Jack lose his temper was when he would lose at poker occasionally, "Arndt said, laughing. "We'd always give the guy who won a courtesy joke – some good ribbing. Jack was always good at that."

For 28 years, Arndt traveled each year to Florida with Buck for spring training, often bringing his family along.

"I used to drive Jack around like a taxi," Arndt said. "When he traveled, I'd take him to the airport, but he never trusted my driving, so he would always drive my car. I'd say, "Jack, I've never been in a fatal accident." But he would insist on driving.

Arndt, born and raised in St. Louis, attended Soldan High School and worked as a regional sales manager for Kaylord Container Corporation.

Upstairs in his den, Arndt keeps several books of poetry by Buck. A poem titled "Remember Me," about World War II is dedicated by Buck to Arndt and his late wife, Alaine. A picture of Arndt and Buck at a bowling tournament in 1994 sits proudly on a bookshelf. "To Joe Arndt," it reads, "Friends forever, Jack Buck."

As the tribute neared an end, Joe Buck appeared on the screen. "There's a special friend of Jack's who couldn't make it today – Joe Arndt – who brought donuts for everyone in the box to each game and is responsible for my having to watch my weight," he said. "We love you, Uncle Joe."

At the sound of his name, Arndt's ears perked and his mouth dropped open. His eyes reddened and he smiled. "They wouldn't let me in there without them!" He joked. "I still have those donuts," he said. "I have two boxes of donuts from Lake Forest Pastry in my freezer right now."

Reporter- Michelle Meyer

Dear Buck family,

My name is Brandon McBride. I am 13 years old and live in Ballwin Missouri. My family and I have sent a sympathy card to you, but I decided to express what I had felt about the loss of a legend. He was the biggest loss to all of St. Louis, and even to all of baseball. Many people may have not known him like myself, but I felt like I had known him all my life. I don't think that any sport club could mend over the hole he left. When he passed he left shoes that nobody could fill. They most likely would be too big for anybody except God. He had filled them with love and compassion. He had been inducted into many Hall of Fames. He had finally been inducted into his happiest Hall of Fame: Everlasting Peace With God. When he would ask God why was he so good to him God would say, " Because you were good to me and my people." He didn't believe in racism. He treated everybody equally. When he entered the stadium he would greet everybody from the general manager to the ushers. If the day was gloomy or somebody was having a bad day seeing his face with that smile or just hearing his voice would cheer them up. When baseball started after September 11th he had made that speech, which made baseball fun to play again. He was one of the biggest editions to the Cardinal baseball clubs. The Cardinal baseball club and all of baseball will always miss him. He is a legend whose story will never end. He is the fire burning within us forever. May God bless you and your family forever.

Sincerely,
Brandon McBride

- - - - - - - - - - - - - - - - - - - -

Dear Mrs. Buck:

On behalf of Barnes-Jewish Hospital, I would like to express our deepest sympathy on the passing of your husband. Mr. Buck was a very special patient for all of us. His humor, dignity, and strength will always be remembered by the people who had an opportunity to care for him. More impressive was the manner in which your family handled his long illness. Your devotion, love and patience were appreciated by everyone. Our entire medical center has learned from this experience. We all share in your loss.

Steven B. Miller, MD

Dear Jack,

One day a couple of years ago I was invited to enjoy Cardinal Baseball in the press box. Although we won the game and Mark McGwire hit a homerun, what brings fondest memories is meeting you. You came up to me, shook my hand and engaged in conversation with me. What a gentleman you are!

I thought it was time to return the favor so thus these warm wishes. I pray that God surrounds you with His love and protection and provides the way for your return to the press box. To hear your voice again will be music to my ears.

Sincerely,
Mary Freshma

— — — — — — — — — — — — — — —

Dear Jack and family,

Like a lot of folks in this area, I am a life-long Cardinal fan. I'm a 43 year old female from Godfrey, Illinois. I'm an only child who felt a responsibility to be a sports fan for my Dad since he didn't have a son. How easy you made baseball for me! I love the game because of you.

Julie

— — — — — — — — — — — — — — —

Dear Jack,

You have inspired me to be a good dad and friend to all.

Jim Heilmann

— — — — — — — — — — — — — — —

I was born in 1954 in Rock Island, Il...Northern Illinois...Cub Territory. But, I was never a Cub fan. I think I have my Dad, Harry Caray, and Jack Buck to thank for that. I, too, went to sleep listening to the Cardinal games on the radio. Jack and Harry really did make the game come alive. The best birthday present I could get was when my parents took me to a Cardinal game. It was a five hour drive! I always take my radio to the games to listen to Jack, Joe, and Mike call the game.

Barbara Hines

To the Buck Family,

I just wanted to share with you a special moment when my daughters Lauren and Kristen Bradley got to meet Jack at a Cardinal baseball game two (2) years ago. After that Cardinal game, I had taken Lauren and Kristen up to where John Mosbacher works (replay board) and he was showing the girls how everything works, etc. It was time to leave and John said you can ride down on the elevator with me. As we got on the elevator Mr. Buck was on the elevator and John whispered to my oldest daughter, "Do you know who this man is?" And she said, "Yes, that's the man who broadcasts the game.
At that time I spoke up and asked Mr. Buck, "Would you be willing to autograph the girls' baseball hats?" And his reply was, "I sure would." So, when we got off the elevator, we stepped into the lobby and he asked them about the game and made some small talk with them and signed their hats.

Kathy Bradley

— —

Anna was indeed a huge Cardinal and Jack Buck fan. The Cardinals had always been a part of her life—from being a part of the Knot-hole Gang at Sportsman Park to her last years as a widow, living alone. I recall my mother being obligated to attend a function at the MAC. It was the playoffs in 1987. She reluctantly went...but not without her little radio.

She "listened" attentively to the speaker with her radio earpiece on the game. The speaker spoke louder and louder sensing my mom was missing his message. When he finally realized it was not a hearing aid—he asked her to break in whenever the Cardinals scored!

Linda Bridges

— —

Dear Mr. Buck,

I have been listening to you since I was 8 years old in 1964. You are the greatest announcer I have ever heard. I have a great deal of respect and affection for you.

Terry M. Killian, M.D.

September 30, 2002
Dear Joe and Mrs. Buck,

     The Cardinals are dedicating their season to Darryl Kile and Jack Buck, and to their families. I would like to thank your father, Joe, and your husband, Mrs. Buck, through this letter, for helping me create memories that have developed feelings and attitudes about sports and life itself.

     When Jack passed away, I was in Washington, D.C., with my wife, baby-sitting our two granddaughters. It was impossible for me to get back to St. Louis without creating a hardship for her. Being in Washington, 'alone', away from my friends in St. Louis who were mourning his passing also, and being away from the media coverage unable to attend any of the services for your father, Joe, at the ballpark, or at the church, made me very sad. I was reminded that I did not send a 'get well' card or letter to him when he was so sick and I am very sorry for that, Mrs. Buck. I thought about him on every day of his hospital stay and hoped so much that he would be back in the booth with Mike. I had told my closest friends that I dreaded the day Jack passed away, for me and for this city. Never did I imagine that I would not be in St. Louis when he died. These wonderful friends of mine made videotapes for me of the different ceremonies for Jack, and saved the newspapers, but I never thought I would not be able to pay my respects to him like I would want.

     I am 55 years old and grew up in Springfield, Missouri, where I played little league sports for eight years. I have lived in St. Louis since 1971. Baseball is my favorite sport and I have loved the Cardinals my whole life. I have followed them through Jack's broadcasts since I was probably five years old.

     Please know, Mrs. Buck, that your husband was a huge factor in making the Cardinals the great baseball organization it is today and making St. Louis the 'best baseball city' in the United States. He was also one of the top personalities that made KMOX the 'voice of St. Louis'. I loved him and loved the things he promoted, because I knew his ideas and his causes were good and right.

     I was lucky enough one evening, maybe three years ago, to visit with Jack at the intermission of a St. Louis Symphony concert. He was standing alone at a small table, on the second level, right above the lobby. As I am sure you have heard so many times in the past, this famous man made me feel like I was the important one in the conversation. He made me feel so good and comfortable that it had not been a bother to him for me to take a bit of his time. It was a wonderful couple of minutes that I will never forget. I was also fortunate to hear him speak at a bank convention in December about ten years ago. I attended Jack Buck day at the ballpark and have a few pictures I took during the ceremony showing Joe and Jack hugging. I am sure you will never forget that day, Joe. It was said there were more than 10,000 people standing outside the stadium watching the unveiling of Jack's statue.

     If I may digress here for just a bit. Joe, I hope you are aware that only you could fill the shoes of Jack Buck behind that Cardinal microphone. And the reason is not because you are his son. The reason is because you are the best. You are the best announcer that has sat in that seat since Jack Buck. And in that seat is where you belong. I realize you have many other obligations right now, but always know that the people who love Cardinal baseball and love KMOX know that it would help keep the 'spirit of St. Louis' alive if you eventually became 'the voice of the Cardinals'.

May I tell you, Joe, my favorite call of a Cardinal's moment by you? It was the opening day of a season and I think your first regular season radio broadcast. I am sure you remember Ray Lankford colliding with another team's catcher at home plate, scoring the winning run for the Cardinals, and your description of the play. Your voice cracked with emotion as you gave it your all.

It was an awesome call. Speaking of calls, I am upset that other announcers are now using your call of "at the track, at the wall…". You are the first announcer I think, to ever use that description and I loved it, but now it seems like everyone is saying it.

I will always be sad that I was not able to be in St. Louis to pay my respects to a man I loved and to his wonderful family. Thank you for giving me these moments to share my feelings about the man we all miss so much. The way he lived his life will always be a model to which I will always strive. I was telling a friend tonight that I had to write this letter for myself; to say good-bye to Jack; yes, I guess, for 'closure'. I pray that my mind will stay healthy long into my years so that I might remember what this brilliant yet humble man brought to my life from ages five to fifty-five. God bless you and your family Mrs. Buck.

> *Very respectfully,*
> *Mike Latimer*

— —

The saddest day in Cardinal history. On June 18, 2002, the heart of every fan in the Cardinal Nation was broken. Many lost a hero, a familiar voice and face, and a role model. This event touches me deep in my heart and makes me only think of 1985 when Ozzie Smith hit his first left handed home run and all of the Dodgers hopes were sunk in a sea of red and finished with a "Go crazy folks!" At the age of six months I do not remember this call as it came live, but the passion and excitement of an announcer's voice, who was supposed to be neutral, gives me chills to the spine.

This team lost one of its greatest icons and will never be able to replace him. The pain in every St. Louis resident and the ones at heart will be immense and not easily forgotten. This man captivated many and gave hope to some when the home team would get into a tough spot with the bases loaded and would say, "This would be the perfect time for a triple play" knowing in his heart he loved the men with the bat and birds on their chests more than anyone could think of. His pride for country and its people were very evident when Major League Baseball resumed play in the wake on the terrorist attacks this September when he recited a poem written by himself on national TV. His poetry was inspiring and described the way every American felt at the time.

Jack Buck's mic will be forever empty and so will the hearts of my fellow Cardinal fans and I will have a void so gaping I could never be filled. Jack Buck will be dearly missed and never forgotten.

> *Steve Lampe*

Dr. John Mahoney
Maureen Mahoney, Jack
At BallBQ Grants Farm 1989

Jack and Diane
January 2001

*F*or the Jack Buck family,

Although I never had the privilege of meeting Jack Buck personally, he was welcomed in our home night after night. My father worked shift work, so he was not able to listen to Jack as much as my mother and I, but the evenings he was home, that was our treat! We would all sit on the front porch and listen to the ballgame.

Mr. Buck brought so much joy and helped to make so many fond memories in our home not only through baseball but through the sharing of our family times on the porch. It was so great to all sit and listen to the play by play and his stories. He had such a gift and a love of people. We hardly ever watched the game—who needed to—Jack drew such a vivid and exciting picture of the game.

You knew you never missed a moment through his words. His strong and enthusiastic voice kept your interest high and longing for his next broadcast once the game was over. Rain delays were great! He will truly be missed but never forgotten as he will remain much alive in our hearts.

Thank you so much for allowing us to be such a big part of his life and for your grace in allowing us to participate in his memorial. God bless and keep you in His loving arms.

Debi Northway

- -

I ADORE JACK AND HE IS ONE OF THE MAIN REASONS I BECAME INTERESTED AND AM NOW PURSUING MY INTEREST IN BROADCASTING. I WOULD LOVE TO MODEL MY LIFE AFTER JACK BECAUSE WHEN I REMEMBER WHO HE WAS AND THE GREAT THINGS HE HAS DONE, I CAN TRULY SAY, "THAT'S A WINNER."

MIKE RICHTER

- -

I grew up on a family farm near Springfield, Ill. I helped my Dad by driving a tractor in the fields when I was in my teens and early twenties. The highlight of the day was the anticipation and the listening of you and Mike on the radio. Listening to you guys is like reading a good novel (especially if the Cardinals win). I'm still listening in Texas.

Louie Trutter

Dear Carole,

I am so incredibly sorry for your loss. Having been married to someone for over three decades is of itself such a blessing, and I know you are a very strong woman, but I also know your heart is hurting. Having had the opportunity to meet you and Jack and see how much you meant to each other was wonderful.

Having grown up listening to Jack and Harry, when I first met him through the Foundation I was completely awed. I have never been one to be very impressed by celebrities and don't collect autographs. When I was the General Manager of the (then) Hotel Majestic, we had so many famous people as our guests, I guess it just reinforced my jadedness. George Stephans had arranged lunch with Jack, and I was surprised at how nervous I was. When I called my mom to tell her I was having lunch with Jack, knowing I have always been somewhat of a smart-mouth, her words to me were "Patricia Jane, you behave yourself. This is JACK BUCK you're going to eat with." She was right—it was JACK BUCK. When I think of how lucky I was to get to know him the past two years, and see his soft heart, his wonderful sense of humor and the way he treated everyone he came in contact with like they were the most important person he was talking to that day, I realized what a gift we had all been given. We were so fortunate that he had someone so special as his wife. I can only imagine how many days/nights/weeks he was gone with his job, and how many issues and crises you had to deal with. You and your children gave up so much of him for all of us, whether as a sports fan or someone with a charity, and we could never thank you enough. I think perhaps God sent Jack to all of us to raise the bar. I saw how people reacted when he walked in; at the golf meetings, all those important "suits" suddenly were sitting straighter, smiling more and trying harder. When he would show up in our office, the whole staff became one huge smile—"Jack's here!" When he would reach in his pocket and pull out a piece of paper with a new poem he would read, it was really the highlight of our week.

Baseball is different for me this year. I guess having die-hard Cards fans as parents, it was just always part of my life. Throughout all the players and coaches and managers, the one constant was Jack. It was always the voice you could count on. Sort of like comfort food for the soul. Things at CF will forever be different now too. As with baseball, Jack was always there for us. Throughout all the board members, executive directors and new staff, he was the one constant. We still find ourselves talking as if he isn't gone. We alternate laughing about something he said to us and then crying because we won't hear his "Hello, hello, hello!" as he walked in the door. One of my most cherished memories is when he and I were talking and I said something that made him chuckle. I made Jack Buck laugh! I was so proud of myself!

I hope you know how much Jack meant to everyone associated with CF. To have had him helping for so very many years and raising so much money to end this disease is truly remarkable. I know there are children living longer lives today because of his help. Thank you for your help, too, Carole. I know you probably ate more chicken dinners at banquets than one person should have to. You always let him help, you always shared him, you always protected him. We will be forever grateful to you for that.

Pat Voight

— — — — — — — — — — — — — — — — — —

Dear Carole,

During the inspiring memorial at Busch Stadium in which the entire Greater St. Louis area demonstrated our respect and love for Jack, our hearts ached for you and your wonderful family.

However, Friday morning, driving to my dealership, when I heard Christina and Joe's eulogy at the church service, I actually broke down and cried.

I takes strong, noble parents like you and Jack to raise such an exemplary, courageous family.

May God bless you and continue to give you the strength in the days ahead that you so lovingly and unselfishly demonstrated during Jack's final illness.

Sincerely,

John and Sylvia Londoff

Cardinal fan sent this picture in while Jack was in the hospital.
"Say, Hi to Jack!"

Thank you for your prayers.
The Wright Triplets
Max, Alec, Danielle

Memorial Day 2001
The Pundmann's with Mr. Buck

CONCLUSION

Jack made a difference....to show us we could make a difference. We will not waste his life. The seed he invested in each of our hearts will sprout to make a difference....maybe even a difference we will never see in our lifetime....due to our focus on others. There were many days Jack was tired and worn. His love for us would not quit.

Jack spent his life saying, "I'm no different than you are. No matter who you are, you write important messages upon people's hearts. Pay attention to everyone regardless of class, color, or conflict." You....you begin to level the playing field right where you are regardless of hurt or setback or imagined disadvantage. Set your needs aside. Give yourself away and see if abundant life doesn't come back a hundred-fold.

I think about one of the great Bible stories when I think about the life and influence of Jack Buck. It was none other than the Son of God who told of the three travelers passing along a dusty road in ancient of days. Two were highly visible religious leaders in the community. The third was not known for his "churchiness". Jesus then sets the stage of the three men making their journey.....one at a time. Each notices the same victim in the ditch. He has been beaten and robbed.

Separately, the first of the two religious leaders looked at the battered one and passed by him going out of his way to avoid contact with the one in desperate need. The second man of public faith, likewise, avoided connection with the stranger. He went on his way to perform his religious deeds while leaving the bleeding man to die.

The third man...the unexpected one.....came along, saw the situation, got down in the ditch with the victim, carried him to a small motel, paid the stranger's room and board and came back to check on him. Jesus then raises the question: "Which of these three do you think proved to be a neighbor to the man who fell into the robbers' hands?" And he said, "The one who showed mercy." And Jesus said to him, "Go and do the same."

That's the story of Jack Buck. He did not parade his faith. He got dirty. He lunged into the abyss of the suffering and crying of others. He was not too clean to touch those who were less fortunate. He was not self-conscious of what others might think. The man abandoned his own comfort zone to see that many who had been abused in some way found that at least one man cared.

If I could have one prayer today,
This only would it be….
That I could live as Jack Buck lived
With love and humility.

And if I could have a second prayer,
This also would it be…
That I could die as Jack Buck died
With love and dignity

Cheryl Fowler

116

....AND ONE YEAR LATER......

Carole passed by Jack's statue at the stadium and noticed someone had the kindness to place a single flower upon his hand. She took great delight in knowing a fan had expressed continued love. It meant so much to her.

Too, she found a note held by a stick in the ground at the grave.

Mr. Buck,

I wanted to remember you this day, the one year anniversary of your death. As I come here to honor my own Mom and Dad during my visit, I often come to be near you, and just sit. I miss you Mr. Buck....all your class, your charm and your wit. To listen to you in the booth was a summer-long joy. I'm remembering your poem from Normandy, France and your touching story about a boy named Lance.

Thank you, Mr. Buck, for all that you believed in. And, thank you again for all you stood for. As I now stand ever closer to where you rest. I thank God for your life, your zeal, your zest. And I must say, "Looky there, looky there!" "There lies a Winner, beneath that stone at which I stare!"

May God bless and cradle you forever,

Craig Marchand

Thank you, fans......you continue to give your hearts away....and you make a difference.

Jack.....you will definitely be missed...but we will always hear your voice.
Rob Fischer

"A Fond Farewell"

The "Voice of the Cardinals" is silent
The light of St. Louis has gone out:
But you set such a good example, Jack
That your fire will never burn out!

Your voice has been stilled
By the grace of God's will
You angels all stopped to bow!

Lord knows, we St. Louisans loved you!
We're so proud that you were our own!
so...so long for awhile, Jack
We'll miss you like crazy,
But your legacy will live on and on!

Anonymous fan

118

The Voice

Smooth as caramel candy, cool as a Drewes' Concrete
The Voice
whisked you from sofa to box seat
when you never moved.

The Voice
equal parts popcorn and popups
hot dogs and home runs
compassion and cotton candy
leather and licorice gravel and green grass

The Voice
from a man and a legend
poet and patriot
soldier and citizen
father and friend
was courage and courtesy
wisdom and wisecracks
warmth and cool confidence.

The Voice
taught from Musial to McGwire
Gibby, Ozzie and Brock
We went crazy
watched in awe couldn't believe what we just saw
stood and applauded
The Voice
made us all winners.

Now in sorrow when body and spirit join ethereal plain but
The Voice
with us, will forever remain.

Kevin McCarney

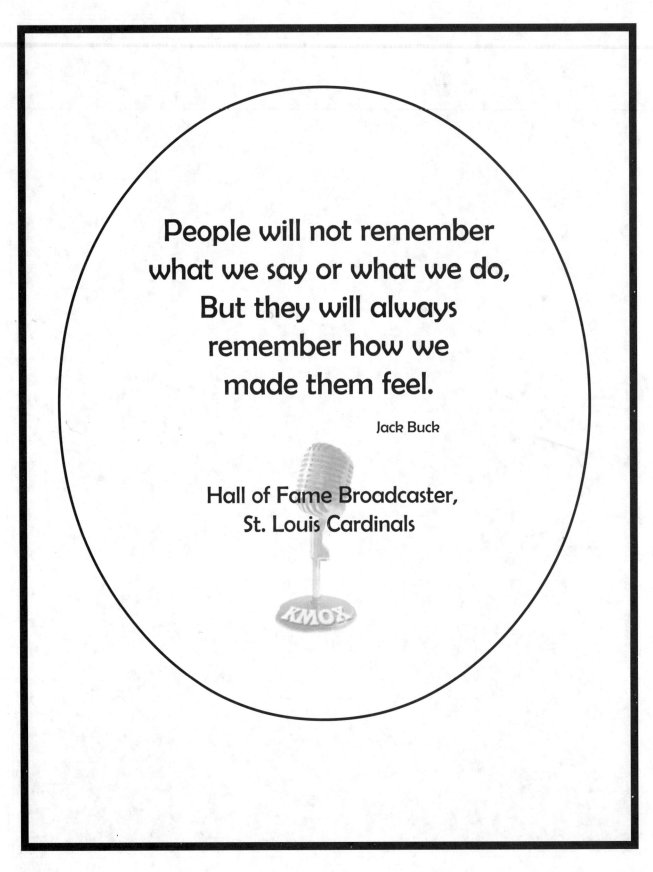

People will not remember
what we say or what we do,
But they will always
remember how we
made them feel.

Jack Buck

Hall of Fame Broadcaster,
St. Louis Cardinals